England's Number Ones

ENGLAND'S NUMBER ONES

Dean Hayes

Aureus

First Published 2000

Cover photographs: David Seaman (England v Moldova) ©John Babb (Prosport); Peter Shilton (England v Germany, 1990) ©Michael Steele (Prosport).
Back cover: Ray Clemence ©Tommy Hindley (Prosport).

ISBN 1 899750 57 6

Printed in Great Britain.

A catalogue record for this book is available from the British Library.

Aureus Publishing Limited, 24 Mafeking Road, Cardiff, CF23 5DQ, UK.
Tel: (029) 2045 5200 Fax: (029) 2045 5200
Int. tel: +44 29 2045 5200 Int. fax: +44 29 2045 5200
E-mail: sales@aureus.co.uk
          meuryn.hughes@aureus.co.uk
Web site: www.aureus.co.uk

INTRODUCTION

Goals are what football is all about. And the great ones, like great occasions, live long in the memory, stored away in the mind to be re-lived and re-told again and again. But if there is one facet of the game which captivates the onlooker as much, it is 'the great save'. The ball speeds goalwards but in the very moment that the roar reaches a crescendo, a palm or a finger tip stretches to divert it away. And in that moment, one hero replaces another.

Every goalkeeper has his day and since their first official international match in 1872, England have had 97 custodians. They form an extremely varied gallery ranging from leading figures in politics, church and the armed forces to the more unusual, the British High Jump champion, a blacksmith's apprentice and a coffee planter from Sri Lanka !

This book I hope captures the flavour of those players who have been England's Number Ones.

Dean P. Hayes
Preston
May 2000

A

JACK ALDERSON

Born	28 November 1891, Crook, Co Durham
Died	17 February 1972
Career	Crook Town; Shildon Athletic; Middlesbrough (cs 1912) Newcastle United (May 1913) Crystal Palace (May 1919) Pontypridd (cs 1924) Sheffield United (May 1929) Exeter City (May 1929) Torquay United (cs 1930) Crook Town (March 1931)
Internationals	1923 v France (Won 4-1)

Jack Alderson began his career with his home-town team followed by a brief spell with Shildon Amateurs before moving to Middlesbrough in the close season of 1912. He remained an amateur at Ayresome Park but unable to make the grade, was transferred to Newcastle United for £50. After turning professional, he finally made his league debut in January 1913 in the Magpies' 3-1 home win over Woolwich Arsenal. However, it turned out to be his only league appearance prior to the outbreak of the First World War as he had tough competition from two other professional 'keepers at Gallowgate, Sid Blake and William Mellor.

During the hostilities he was posted to Woolwich and in January 1919 he signed for Crystal Palace. He made his debut in the London War League when Palace lost 6-1 to Brentford but despite this setback, he quickly became something of a legend. Alderson did not miss a game when league football resumed in 1919 until February 1922 and was ever-present in the Eagles' championship-winning season of 1920-21, the initial Third Division campaign.

Alderson was noted for his ability to stop penalties - he had the amazing record of saving 11 out of 12 penalties including two in the match against Bradford City at Valley Parade.

After winning an England cap against France in May 1923, Alderson was involved in a pay dispute at Palace and left to play non-League football for Pontypridd before returning to league action with Sheffield United in May 1925. He made 122 league appearances for the Blades before joining Exeter City in the summer of 1929. After 36 league appearances for the Grecians, Alderson was forced to retire.

He later had a spell on the training staff of Torquay United before returning to play for Crook where he combined playing with work as a farmer.

RUPERT ANDERSON

Born	29 April 1859. Liverpool
Died	23 December 1944

Career	Eton College (XI 1878) Cambridge University, Old Etonians.
Internationals	1879 v Wales (won 2-1)

A member of the 1878 Eton College XI, he went on to Cambridge University but did not win a Blue. On joining Old Etonians, Anderson became a zealous and lively forward but was a goalkeeper in his sole international appearance as England beat Wales 2-1 at Kennington Oval. On returning to Old Etonians, Anderson turned in a series of impressive displays to help his club reach the FA Cup Final but was sadly forced to miss the game in which Old Etonians beat Clapton Rovers 1-0, through injury.

On retirement, Anderson went to work as an orange planter in Florida, for some time residing in Staffordshire and at Wavereley Abbey, Farnham, Surrey on his return to England.

During the First World War he was awarded the OBE for his services to the Territorial Army and the Royal Air Force.

HERBIE ARTHUR

Born	14 February 1863. Blackburn.
Died	27 November 1930
Career	Lower Bank Academy(Blackburn) King's Own FC (Blackburn) Blackburn Rovers (cs 1880) Southport Central (cs 1890)
Internationals	1885 v Ireland (Won 4-0) v Wales (Drew 1-1) v Scotland (Drew 1-1) 1886 v Wales (Won 3-1) v Scotland (Drew 1-1) 1887 v Ireland (Won 7-0) v Wales (Won 4-0)

One of the most reliable goalkeepers in Blackburn Rovers' history, Herbie Arthur played his early football with local clubs Lower Bank Academy and King's Own before turning out for the Ewood Park club. Arthur joined the club as a wing-half in 1880 but in April 1882 he volunteered to keep goal for Rovers' reserve side.

Arthur was a member of a local well-to-do business family and employment in the family business as a mill furnisher kept him out of the professionalism debate which was raging at that time.

As a goalkeeper, Arthur preferred to rely on positional play rather than produce spectacular leaps to keep his goal intact. He rose to prominence in the mid 1880s, helping Rovers win the FA Cup in 1883-84, 1884-85 and 1885-86. His form led to him representing Lancashire in county matches and winning seven full caps for England, the first against Ireland in 1885.

However, by the time the Football League was founded in 1888, Arthur was no longer in his prime, though he did make his debut in the club's first game in the competition - a 5-5 home draw against Accrington ! Midway through the season, a serious knee injury in the 5-2 defeat of Notts County kept him out of action and over the next couple of campaigns, his appearances were restricted.

In 1891 he left Ewood Park to play for Southport Central but with Rovers' regular 'keepers Pennington and Horne injured, he was brought back to Blackburn for the 1891-92 season but only on the understanding that he was made captain !

On 12 December 1891, Herbie Arthur had a peculiar experience in the game at Burnley. During a memorable blizzard, the rest of the Blackburn side had left the field half-frozen and blinded with the sleet - but Arthur stayed on to hold the fort against the whole Burnley team. A lot of ludicrous stories of what happened were circulated but when the referee ordered the game to proceed and Burnley kicked-off, Arthur at once claimed offside. The referee allowed the appeal but Arthur hesitated so long in taking the free-kick that the official wisely declared the game at an end !

JAMES ASHCROFT

Born	12 September 1878. Liverpool.
Died	9 April 1943
Career	Garston Copper Works(Liverpool) Gravesend United (cs 1899) Woolwich Arsenal (May 1900) Blackburn Rovers (May 1908) Tranmere Rovers (cs 1913)
Internationals	1906 v Ireland (Won 5-0) v Wales (Won 1-0) v Scotland (Lost 1-2)

James Ashcroft began his career with several Liverpool youth sides and for a short time was on the books of Everton before joining Southern League club Gravesend United in 1899. After a series of impressive performances, he was transferred to Woolwich Arsenal in June 1900 where he immediately gained a first team position, replacing Thomas Spicer in the club's third game of the 1900-01 season against Burton.

He kept his place for the rest of the season and in 1901-02 was ever-present, helping the Gunners to their then highest-ever league position of fourth in Division Two. During that campaign, Ashcroft established a club record which is still held today when his total of 17 clean sheets included a run of six games without conceding a goal. In 1920-03 he helped the club to third place in Division Two and was ever-present again the following season when the Gunners won promotion, keeping 20 clean sheets.

His run of 154 consecutive league games ended when he missed a game early in the 1904-05 season, though he returned to play in the remaining matches. In 1905-06 he was instrumental in helping the Gunners reach the FA Cup semi-final and after winning Football League representative honours, he won three full caps for England.

In 1906-07 he helped Woolwich Arsenal reach the FA Cup semi-finals but at the end of the following season after appearing in 303 League and Cup games, he was transferred to Blackburn Rovers.

In five seasons with the Ewood Park club, Ashcroft appeared in 129 games, helping Rovers to the FA Cup semi-finals in 1910-11. The following season he lost his place midway through the campaign due to ill-health and so missed out on a League Championship medal. In 1913 he moved to Tranmere Rovers where he ended his playing career.

GEORGE ASHMORE

Born	5 May 1898. Plymouth
Died	19 May 1973
Career	South Devon Schools. Nineveh Wesley (Handsworth League) West Bromwich Albion (November 1919) Chesterfield (October 1931)
Internationals	1926 v Belgium (Won 5-3)

Plymouth-born goalkeeper George Ashmore represented South Devon and District Schools before moving with his family to the Midlands. He was playing in the Handsworth League for Nineveh Wesley when West Bromwich Albion spotted his potential in November 1919 and signed him on professional forms.

Despite making his Albion debut against Blackburn Rovers in October 1920, a match the Baggies lost 5-1, Ashmore was in the shadow of Harold Pearson for a number of years and it wasn't until 1923-24 that he became the club's first-choice goalkeeper.

In May 1926, Ashmore won his one and only England cap when he played against Belgium in Antwerp. In a match England won 5-3, Frank Osborne scored a hat-trick and Joe Carter, one of Ashmore's Albion team-mates, scored one of the other goals. An agile and daring goalkeeper, George Ashmore was a loyal clubman, appearing in 268 League and Cup games for Albion. The last of these appearances came in March 1930 against Cardiff City, after which the 'keeper known as 'Cat' moved to play for Chesterfield.

A regular in his two seasons at Saltergate, Ashmore retired in the summer of 1933 and went to work for the Midlands Electricity Board.

B

TOM BADDELEY

Born	2 November 1874. Bycars nr Burslem.
Died	24 September 1946
Career	Burslem Swifts (May 1890) Burslem Port Vale (May 1892) Wolverhampton Wanderers (October 1896) Bradford Park Avenue (May 1907) Stoke (1910)
Internationals	1903 v Ireland (Won 4-0) v Scotland (Lost 1-2) 1904 v Wales (Drew 2-2) v Ireland (Won 3-1) v Scotland (Won 1-0)

Tom Baddeley who was born at Bycars near Burslem, Stoke-on-Trent in November 1874, was an unspectacular goalkeeper - yet he was very safe, being both calm and courageous on the pitch. He began his career with Burslem Swifts in 1890 before joining Burslem Port Vale in 1892. He became a regular in the Vale side from September 1894 and was ever-present during the 1894-95 and 1895-96 seasons but was suspended in the summer of 1896 after signing a second professional form for another club !

In October 1896, Baddeley was sold to Wolverhampton Wanderers for £50. Able to deal with any type of shot, he was agile and brave and commanded his area well, having an excellent long kick and indeed could throw a ball out from anything up to 50 yards, which was unusual in those days.

After making his league debut in a 3-0 win over Preston North End, Baddeley went on to spend eleven years at Molineux, playing in 315 League and Cup games. His form led to him winning five full international caps for England and representing the Football League on four occasions. He lined up against Ireland and Scotland in 1903 and Wales, Ireland and

Scotland in 1904. He let in five goals in those internationals, keeping two clean sheets in his first and last outings.

In May 1907, Baddeley left Molineux to become one of newly-formed Bradford Park Avenue's first signings. By the time he left the Yorkshire club, three seasons later, they were a well established Second Division club.

In March 1910 Baddeley joined Stoke as with Jack Robinson indisposed, the Potters' directors brought him to the Victoria Ground. Playing in the remaining Birmingham League fixtures, he kept four clean sheets in the seven games in which he appeared before deciding to retire at the end of the season.

GARY BAILEY

Born	9 August 1958. Ipswich.
Career	Witts University (South Africa) Manchester United (January 1978) retired through injury April 1987.
Internationals	1985 v Republic of Ireland (Won 2-1)
	v Mexico (Lost 0-1)

The son of Roy Bailey, the former Ipswich Town goalkeeper, Gary was living in South Africa and playing for Witts University when he was sent to Old Trafford for a trial by former Manchester United player, Eddie Lewis in January 1978. He made his league debut for the Reds in November that year, coincidentally against Ipswich Town, a match United won 2-0. When United played West Bromwich Albion the following month, Tony Brown netted twice in the Baggies 5-3 win at Old Trafford and in doing so, created a piece of Football League history - it was the only known instance of the same player scoring past both father and son - he netted past Roy during Ipswich Town's League Championship-winning season of 1961-62 !

Bailey ended his first season as United's 'keeper with an FA Cup Final appearance where he was bitterly disappointed not to cut out a cross from Graham Rix which allowed Alan Sunderland to score Arsenal's winning goal. More FA Cup Final appearances followed as United beat Brighton and Hove Albion in 1983 and Everton in 1985.

After 14 appearances for the England Under-21 side, Bailey was rewarded with his first full cap for his country against the Republic of Ireland in

March 1985, a match England won 2-1. Bailey began to suffer from a bad knee injury sustained while training with the England squad in February 1986 and at the age of twenty-nine, was eventually forced to retire, having made 373 League and Cup appearances for Manchester United. He returned to live in South Africa where he later resumed his playing career with Kaiser Chiefs. In December 1989 he decided to retire from football to take up a job as a television commentator while still coaching soccer.

HORACE BAILEY

Born	3 July 1881. Derby
Died	1 August 1960
Career	Derby County Reserves (1899-1902) before joining Ripley Athletic, continuing to assist Derby reserves on occasion; Leicester Imperial to 1905; Leicester Fosse (cs 1906) Derby County (April 1909) Stoke (October 1910) Birmingham (February 1911-1913)
Internationals	1908 v Wales (won 7-1) v Austria (Won 6-1) v Austria (Won 11-1) v Hungary (Won 7-0) v Bohemia (Won 4-0)

Horace Bailey or 'HP' as he was known was a brilliant amateur goalkeeper who throughout his playing years was employed by the Midland Railway Company at Derby as a rating official. Bailey was not big by goalkeeping standards yet dealt with all kinds of shots capably and sometimes brilliantly. He began his career with Derby County but on being unable to break into the first team, assisted Ripley Athletic. He later had a spell with Leicester Imperial before joining Leicester Fosse where he had his greatest success.

He gained near-immediate full international recognition for his valuable contribution to Fosse's promotion-winning side of 1907-08 - thereby becoming the club's first England cap. 'HP' climaxed that busy year of 1908 by also appearing for the victorious United Kingdom XI in the football final of the Olympic Games. A year later he was the blameless last-line of defence during Fosse's record 12-0 defeat at Nottingham Forest and also one of two players to give satisfactory evidence at the subsequent League enquiry. His departure after collecting five senior and four amateur caps while with Fosse, was solely aimed at helping the Rams out of an injury crisis.

However, Stoke's England international 'keeper Jack Robinson was ill and in the autumn of 1910, Stoke's directors searched for a replacement and signed Horace Bailey. Although he only signed for a short spell, it was a scoop for the club. The newspapers advised the supporters that he was an older player and they were pleasantly surprised when he turned out to be twenty-nine - Robinson was almost forty-five at this time. He made just one appearance for Stoke before joining Birmingham where after playing in 53 games, he retired shortly before the outbreak of the First World War.

HOWARD BAKER

Born	13 February 1892. Aigburth, Liverpool
Died	10 September 1987

Career	Marlborough Old Boys, Liverpool Balmoral, Northern Nomads. Assisted the Corinthians from 1920-21 for more than a decade. Also Blackburn Rovers (pre-First World War) Preston North End (December 1919) Liverpool (1920) Everton (1920-21 and 1926-27) Chelsea (October 1921-1926) and Oldham Athletic (1928-29)
Internationals	1921 v Belgium (Won 2-0) 1925 v Ireland (Drew 0-0)

B. Howard Baker as he is often shown in team line-ups, was one of the great characters of inter-war soccer. He was an agile goalkeeper, one who was always popular with spectators, though he had earlier played at centre-half and indeed represented Lancashire and had an amateur international trial in that position.

Howard Baker was born in Liverpool in February 1892 and his career took him to several league clubs as an amateur. Besides the famous amateur clubs Northern Nomads and Corinthians, Baker also played for Blackburn Rovers, Everton (where he was first capped) Chelsea (where he was capped again) and Oldham Athletic, clocking up 106 league appearances in the process.

In the days when goalkeepers never strayed out of their penalty areas, it was a remarkable sight to see Baker sometimes dash upfield with the ball at his feet.

Baker was also a renowned athlete, representing Great Britain at the Olympic Games of 1912 and 1920 in the high jump event. He was the AAA high-jump champion and British record holder at 6ft 5ins - a record achieved at Huddersfield in June 1921 and one that stood for twenty-six years.

Baker also played cricket for Liverpool CC, was international standard at water polo and excelled at the hurdles and throwing discus. Without doubt, an all-rounder to rank with C.B.Fry and Max Woosnam !

GORDON BANKS

Born	30 December 1937. Sheffield
Career	Sheffield Schools, Millspout Steel Works, Chesterfield (September 1955) Leicester City (May 1959) Stoke City (April 1967) retired through eye injury sustained in road accident. Became Port Vale reserve team coach (December 1978 - December 1979) Telford United general manager (January - September 1980) Spell as Stoke City goalkeeping coach from February 1982.
Internationals	1963 v Scotland (Lost 1-2) v Brazil (Drew 1-1) v Czechoslovakia (Won 4-2) v E.Germany (Won 2-1) v Wales (Won 4-0) v Rest of World (Won 2-1) v N.Ireland (Won 8-3) 1964 v Scotland (Lost 0-1) v Uruguay (Won 2-1) v Portugal (Won 4-3) v USA (Won 10-0) v Portugal (Drew 1-1) v Argentina (Lost 0-1) v N.Ireland (Won 4-3) 1965 v Scotland (Drew 2-2)v Hungary (Won 1-0) v Yugoslavia (Drew 1-1) v W.Germany (Won 1-0) v Sweden (Won 2-1) v N.Ireland (Won 2-1) v Spain (Won 2-0) 1966 v Poland (Drew 1-1) v W.Germany (Won 1-0) v Scotland (Won 4-3) v Yugoslavia (Won 2-0) v Finland (Won 3-0) v Poland (Won 1-0) v Uruguay (Drew 0-0) v Mexico (won 2-0) v France (Won 2-0) v Argentina (Won 1-0) v Portugal (Won 2-1) v W.Germany (Won 4-2) v N.Ireland (Won 2-0) v Czechoslovakia (Drew 0-0) v Wales (Won 5-1) 1967 v Scotland (Lost 2-3) v Wales (Won 3-0) v N.Ireland (Won 2-0) v Soviet Union (Drew 2-2) 1968 v Scotland (Drew 1-1) v Spain (Won 1-0) v W.Germany (Lost 0-1) v Yugoslavia (Lost 0-1) v Soviet Union (Won 2-0) v Romania (Drew 0-0) 1969 v Romania (Drew 1-1) v France (Won 5-0) v N.Ireland (Won 3-1) v Scotland (Won 4-1) v Uruguay (Won 2-1) v Brazil (Lost 1-2) 1970 v Holland (Drew 0-0) V Belgium (Won 3-1) v Wales (Drew 1-1) v N.Ireland (Won 3-1) v Scotland (Drew 0-0) v Colombia (Won 4-0) v Ecuador (Won 2-0)

v Romania (Won 1-0) v Brazil (Lost 0-1)
v Czechoslovakia (Won 1-0) 1971 v Malta (Won 1-0)
v Greece (Won 3-0) v Malta (Won 5-0) v N.Ireland
(Won 1-0) v Scotland (Won 3-1) v Switzerland (Won
3-2) v Greece (Won 2-0) 1972 v W.Germany (Lost 1-3
v W.Germany (Drew 0-0) v Wales (Won 3-0)
v Scotland (Won 1-0)

Arguably, Gordon Banks is the greatest goalkeeper of all-time who in the 1970 World Cup in Mexico, made a save that is repeatedly shown on TV and is claimed to be the best save ever. Whether this is true or not will always be a matter of debate for as long as fans argue about such things but suffice to say it is the greatest televised save and was performed at the highest level. The save was of course from a header from the legendary Pele who it is reported shouted out 'goal' as soon as he headed it, only to witness Banks throw himself to his right and turn the ball over the bar !

Banks was first noticed in Chesterfield's unexpected progress to the FA Youth Cup Final in 1956. He was still a raw youngster when Leicester City manager Matt Gillies signed him for £7,000 after just 23 league games for the Spireites.

At Filbert Street he quickly developed into one of the best 'keepers in the country, basing his game on an uncanny sense of positioning, superb reflexes and agility. He won the first of his 73 caps for England when he played in the 2-1 defeat by Scotland at Wembley in April 1963. The rise to contention of Peter Shilton spelt a controversially premature end to Banks' Leicester City career and in April 1967 he joined Stoke City for a fee of £52,000.

Banks was the man who made goalkeeping glamorous but there was nothing pretentious about him. He was outstanding at his job and accepted the praise with quiet dignity. Even after England's 1966 World Cup final win he remained quite unmoved by the fame. The Banks legend took root at Wembley in 1966 and his success and amiable personality gave a new aura and stature to goalkeeping. Banks was so influential in England's emergence as a world power in football that coaches and managers began to realise that if they wanted to build successful teams, one of their priorities was to find a top quality goalkeeper.

At club level, he inspired Stoke to their first-ever trophy, the League Cup in 1972 as the Potters beat Chelsea 2-1 and earned himself the accolade of

1972 Footballer of the Year. Why 1972 ? Did the football writers have to wait until he was on the winning side in a Wembley final ? Perhaps it was because he had never played for a fashionable club ! Only one other goal-keeper had ever been Footballer of the Year and that was Bert Trautmann of Manchester City in 1956.

Sadly, Gordon Banks' world was shattered on Sunday 22 October 1972, when returning home from the Victoria Ground after treatment, he was involved in a serious road crash that was to cost him the sight of his right eye. Television companies broke into programmes to advise of his accident and progress which became a national story.

He fought hard to regain his position after a long lay off but was unable to make it although he played with great distinction for two seasons in the NASL with Fort Lauderdale Strikers.

After stints of coaching at Stoke and Port Vale and a spell as manager of Telford United, he returned to Filbert Street in 1986 as chairman of the Foxes' short-lived 'Lifeline' fund raising operation. Subsequently he has been involved in the corporate hospitality business and was the beneficiary of a well-attended testimonial game at Filbert Street in April 1995 and a suite in the new main stand bears his name. An immensely likeable man, his consistency was legendary and he simply was the best !

RON BAYNHAM

Born	10 June 1929. Birmingham.
Career	Erdington Rovers (1946) Bromford Amateurs; Worcester City (1949) Luton Town (November 1951) Retired through injury (1965).
Internationals	1955 v Denmark (Won 5-1) v N.Ireland (Won 3-0) v Spain (Won 4-1)

Ron Baynham did not play any competitive football until serving in the army where he was spotted in a semi-final against the Paras. A scout tipped off Wolves manager Stan Cullis and a trial was arranged but Ron rejected it, thinking he was not good enough! After spells playing for Erdington Rovers and Bromford Amateurs, an old friend Arthur Haynes persuaded him to join Worcester City. Within two years he was on his way to Luton Town for a fee of £1,000. After a series of impressive displays for the Hatters' reserve side, he displaced England international 'keeper Bernard Streten for the match against Swansea Town in September 1952 giving a competent performance in a 3-1 win for Luton.

He quickly developed into one of the club's best-ever 'keepers, his judgement and all-round efficiency aided by his height and litheness.

Baynham made his breakthrough at the highest level during the 1955-56 season. He made three appearances in the autumn of 1955, the first coming against Denmark in Copenhagen, a match England won 5-1. Despite the result, he lost his place to Bert Williams but after England went down 2-1 to Wales in their next international, Baynham was recalled for the next two matches, again being on the winning side as Northern Ireland and Spain were beaten at Wembley by scores of 3-0 and 4-1 respectively.

It came as a great shock when he was left out of the party to tour Europe at the end of the season. He had also played for the Football League in an unexpected defeat by the Irish League and this was suggested as the explanation.

Baynham who missed just one game in each of the 1955-5 and 1957-58 seasons, was in goal when Luton lost 2-1 to Nottingham Forest in the FA Cup Final of 1959. Despite relegation the following season, Baynham, who was an extremely brave 'keeper, kept his place until the end of the 1964-65 season when after appearing in 432 games, he was forced to retire through injury. It was later discovered that he had played with part of his pelvic structure pulled away by torn muscles and tendons, a condition which was lucky not to leave him crippled. After a spell as coach to Ampthill, he worked as an interior decorator.

DAVE BEASANT

Born	20 March 1959. Willesden.
Career	Edgware Town; Wimbledon (August 1979) Newcastle United (June 1988) Chelsea (January 1989) Grimsby Town on loan (October 1992) Wolverhampton Wanderers on loan (January 1993) Southampton (November 1993) Nottingham Forest (August 1997)
Internationals	1990 v Italy (Drew 0-0) Yugoslavia (Won 2-1)

Dave Beasant began his career as a prolific scoring centre-forward before switching to between the posts. He was discovered by Wimbledon while playing for Edgware Town and made his debut for the Dons in a 2-1 home defeat by Blackpool in January 1979, afterwards becoming a regular in the Wimbledon side. He did not miss a league game from the beginning of the 1981-82 season until he left for Newcastle United in the summer of 1988, a total of 304 consecutive Football League matches.

During that time, Beasant won a Fourth Division Championship medal and helped the club win promotion to the top flight. He was ever-present in seven seasons for Wimbledon and was voted Player of the Year in 1980-81. The last of his 391 games for the Dons was the sensational 1988 FA Cup Final against Liverpool which saw him save John Aldridge's penalty. It was the first spot-kick saved in Cup Final history at Wembley as the Dons held on to take the trophy back to south London.

It was not a great surprise when he was sold at the end of that season to Newcastle United for £800,000, thus becoming Britain's most expensive 'keeper at that time. Unfortunately it wasn't really the best move for either the player or the Magpies.

During his short stay at St James' Park he had little opportunity to further his reputation and after just six months on Tyneside he was 'rescued' by Chelsea who paid £725,000 for his services.

He helped them win the Second Division Championship and in the summer of 1990 won international recognition when he came on as a substitute goalkeeper for England against Italy. A cracked bone in a finger ended an uninterrupted run of senior appearances stretching back nine years in the autumn of 1990.

The following season a series of niggling injuries allowed Kevin Hitchcock to mount a serious challenge for the goalkeeper's jersey. After a disastrous match against Norwich City in September 1992, Chelsea manager Ian Porterfield told him he would never play for the club again. He had loan spells at Grimsby Town and Wolverhampton Wanderers before joining Southampton for £300,000 in November 1993.

Nicknamed 'Lurch' he went on to make the Number One spot his own after sharing the goalkeeping duties with Bruce Grobbelaar and in 1995-96 was voted the south coast club's Player of the Year. After being loaned to Nottingham Forest when the City Ground club's three 'keepers were all injured and keeping clean sheets in each of his first three games, he was signed on a permanent basis.

In his first season with the club he kept 21 clean sheets and helped them win promotion to the Premier League. Establishing himself as the club's first-choice 'keeper ahead of Welsh international Mark Crossley, he captained the side when Steve Chettle was injured but in the summer of 1999, when reaching the age of 40, he was released.

REGINALD BIRKETT

Born	28 March 1849. London
Died	30 June 1898

Career	Lancing College (XI 1866-67) Lancing Old Boys; Clapham Rovers; also represented Surrey.
Internationals	1879 v Scotland (Won 5-4)

Reginald Birkett first played football for Lancing College where he not only appeared in goal but also in both forward and full-back positions. After a brief spell playing for Lancing Old Boys, he joined Clapham Rovers where his early form led to him winning representative honours for Surrey. A fearless 'keeper with a powerful kick, he was in goal for Clapham Rovers when they lost 1-0 to Old Etonians in the 1879 FA Cup Final but was on the winning side the following year as Clapham defeated Oxford University 1-0.

In April 1879, Birkett had won full international honours for England when he played in the 5-4 defeat of Scotland at Kennington Oval. A match of which one contemporary writer wrote:

'A better football match than that played under Association rules has probably never been witnessed. From the kick-off to the call of time the play was exceedingly fast and the interest was sustained up to the last moment' - unfortunately for Birkett, it was his only appearance at that level.

With John Sutcliffe and Charlie Wilson, Birkett was one of three men honoured by England at both football and rugby union. Indeed, Birkett is a name looming large in early Rugby Union annals and Reginald Birkett, whose brother and son were also rugby union internationals, was a member of the original Rugby Union Committee. After retiring from the playing side of both sports, he worked as a hide and skin broker in the City.

PETER BONETTI

Born   27 September 1941. Putney.

Career   Worthing RC Youth Club, Chelsea (April 1959) retired
                     May 1979 but signed for Dundee United in July, finally
                     retiring cs 1980. Later became a Chelsea coach.

Internationals   1966 v Denmark (Won 2-0) 1967 v Spain (Won 2-0)
                     v Austria (Won 1-0) 1968 v Spain (Won 2-1)
                     1969 v Holland (Won 1-0) v Portugal (Won 1-0)
                     1970 v West Germany (Lost 2-3)

Peter Bonetti's future in professional football was shaped before he left school - on the day in 1957 when his mother wrote to Ted Drake then Chelsea's manager and asked if he would give a trial to her son who 'might make you a useful goalkeeper'. He had that trial in January 1958, joined the Stamford Bridge groundstaff six months later, signed professional forms in April 1959 and made his league debut at home to Manchester City on 2 April 1960.

From then on he was always first-choice. In 1962-63 he helped Chelsea to promotion, in 1964-65 he was in goal when they won the League Cup and in 1967 - the season he was voted Chelsea' first Player of the Year - he made his first appearance at Wembley when Spurs beat them in the FA Cup Final.

Bonetti's daring and spectacular play thrilled the crowds and was a decisive factor in the club's cup triumphs of the early 1970s. In the 1970 FA Cup Final at Wembley, he touched world-class in extra-time to deny Leeds United the victory their superiority deserved and in the replay at Old Trafford, Bonetti allied bravery to brilliance to bring Chelsea back from the brink of disaster after being knocked to the ground in the mid-air collision with Mick Jones. With his left knee badly swollen, Bonetti played for the remaining hour of normal time and through the torture of the extra period. The injury had left him unable to take off for the shot which Jones put Leeds into the lead, but the turning point came at 1-1 when twice in a minute he dived to save fierce shots from Terry Cooper. Without such courage the Cup would never have gone to Chelsea for the first time that night.

The following year in the club's European Cup Winners' Cup triumph in Athens, it was touch and go whether Bonetti would play in the final against Real Madrid because pneumonia had kept him out of the quarter and semi-finals in which John Phillips had proved an admirable deputy. But in

Athens, manager Dave Sexton went for experience. After Chelsea had been shocked by Zoco's 89th minute equaliser, Bonetti produced three superb extra-time saves and Chelsea lived to fight again two nights later. In the replay, Chelsea led 2-0 with just a quarter-of-an-hour to go but a goal by Fleitas revived the Spanish side and the closing minutes belonged to Bonetti. Twice he was off the line to block shots by Amancio and seconds from time came one of his greatest saves when he sprang to the left and clutched Zoco's point-blank header.

Despite these two outstanding performances, sandwiched-in between was one nightmare game - England's defeat by West Germany in the quarter-finals of the 1970 World Cup. England, 2-0 up with only twenty minutes to play, eventually lost to their greatest rivals 3-2 in extra-time and it was Bonetti who bore the brunt of the criticism.

In 1972 he was back at Wembley though when Stoke beat Chelsea 2-1 in the League Cup Final, it meant that he had appeared in three club games at the stadium and never finished on the winning side. Style, grace and the quickest reflexes earned from his team-mates, the nickname of 'The Cat'.

When it was announced in March 1975 that he was to be given a free transfer, it appeared his long association with the club was at an end but after a summer spent playing in American football, he returned to Stam-ford Bridge on a monthly contract, helping Eddie McCreadie's young team win promotion in 1976-77. He continued to battle for a first team place over the next two seasons, taking his total of appearances to 728 before moving to the Isle of Mull in 1979, combining life as a guest-house proprietor with occasional appearances for Dundee United. Since then he has acted as a goalkeeping coach to Chelsea as well as being involved with the England set-up.

JACK BROWN

Born	19 March 1899. Hodthorpe, Derbyshire.
Died	10 April 1962.
Career	Manton Colliery; Worksop Town (1919) Sheffield Wednesday (February 1923) Hartlepool United (September 1937)
Internationals	1927 v Wales (Drew 3-3) v Scotland (Won 2-1) v Belgium (Won 9-1) v Luxembourg (Won 5-2) v France (Won 6-0) 1929 v Ireland (Won 3-0)

This miner-turned goalkeeper began his career with Manton Colliery before linking up with Worksop Town, his local team in 1919. Brown, who became a goalkeeper by accident, having started out as a junior cen-tre-forward, enjoyed a moment of national fame with the non-League club.

In the early part of 1923 he was in the Worksop team that held mighty Tottenham Hotspur to a goalless draw in the first round FA Cup tie at White Hart Lane, although the London club thrashed the Midland League side 9-0 in the replay !

Sheffield Wednesday paid £300 for his services and Brown was delighted to quit working at Manton Colliery. But the Owls' new 'keeper did not immediately displace veteran custodian Teddy Davison and in fact, it was not until the Second Division championship-winning season of 1925-26 that he became the club's number one choice. That season, he was ever-present, keeping 16 clean sheets, going on to be the Owls regular 'keeper for the next twelve seasons.

During that time, he helped the Hillsborough club win two League titles and the FA Cup in 1935 when Wednesday beat West Bromwich Albion 4-2.

Brown, who lacked nothing in courage, won many admirers with his fearlessness and in 1927 won the first of six England caps when he played in the 3-3 draw against Wales at Wrexham. Brown also played twice for the Football League but towards the end of the 1936-37 season, he lost his place in the Owls' side.

In September 1937, Brown, who had appeared in 507 League and Cup games for Sheffield Wednesday joined Hartlepool United, making just one appearance for the north-east club before being released a fortnight later.

C

WILLIAM CARR

Born	15 November 1848. Sheffield.
Died	22 February 1924.
Career	Besides the Sheffield club, he also assisted other clubs in the area - Walkley, Wednesday and Owlerton. Also represented the Sheffield FA.
Internationals	1875 v Scotland (Drew 2-2)

Though most of his playing career was spent with the Sheffield club, William Carr also assisted a number of other local clubs including Walkley, Wednesday and Owlerton. His performances earned him selection for the Sheffield FA and C.W.Alcock in his annual of 1874, says that Carr 'has again and again vindicated his right to the first place among custodians of the goal.' One of the tallest 'keepers of his day, he had great composure and the capacity to judge shots and like a number of other players of his generation, he could perform efficiently in outfield positions too !

In March 1875, Carr, who was at the time Secretary of the Owlerton club, was chosen to represent England in the match against Scotland at Kennington Oval. However, because of the derailment of his train, he was late arriving at the ground and caused England to be one player short for the first quarter-of-an-hour, Bonsor the Wanderers' centre-forward going in goal. Scotland couldn't take advantage of the situation and when Carr appeared, Bonsor returned to lead the forward-line and laid on England's opening goal. The home side extended their lead through captain Charles Alcock before Carr was forced to make a couple of fine saves from McNeill

(Queen's Park) and McPherson (Clydesdale) before being beaten twice in the space of a few minutes late in the game. It was Carr's only appearance for his country and he returned to his home-town of Sheffield where he continued to be involved in local football.

CHRIS CHARSLEY

Born	7 November 1864. Leicester.
Died	10 January 1945.

Career	Stafford Town (1881) Stafford Rangers (during which he 'guested' for Aston Villa) Small Heath (1886) West Bromwich Albion (August 1891) Small Heath (December 1891) retired in 1893 but came out of retirement to assist Small Heath in the Test Matches of 1894.
Internationals	1893 v Ireland (Won 6-1)

Chris Charsley played his early football with Stafford Town and Stafford Rangers but in 1883 he joined the Birmingham police force. He remained an amateur throughout his playing career which revolved around his work as a police officer. After a spell 'guesting' for Aston Villa, Charlsey signed for Small Heath after putting on a quite brilliant display against them whilst playing for Stafford.

Tall with a safe pair of hands and a strong kick, Charsley made his debut for the Blues against Mitchell St George's in an FA Cup tie. By this time, Charlsey had been appointed to the position of chief inspector but he continued to keep goal for the Blues until 1891 when he signed for West Bromwich Albion. Within weeks, he was back at Muntz Street and in 1892-93 helped Small Heath win the Second Division Championship.

That season also saw him win his one full cap for England when he played in a 6-1 win over Ireland at Birmingham. He retired in 1893 but came out of retirement a year later to assist Small Heath in the Test Matches.

On finally leaving the game, he became the Chief Constable of Coventry, a position he held for nineteen years. He then moved to live in Weston-super-Mare where he was elected to the town council, rising to Deputy Mayor in 1939-40 and remaining in office until his death in January 1945.

RAY CLEMENCE

Born   5 August 1948. Skegness.

Career   Skegness Youth Club; Scunthorpe United (August
                 1965) Liverpool (June 1967) Tottenham Hotspur
                 (August 1981) Tottenham Hotspur coach; Barnet
                 Manager (1994-1996) England goalkeeping coach.

Internationals   1972 v Wales (Won 1-0) 1973 v Wales (Drew 1-1) 1974
                 v East Germany (Drew 1-1) v Bulgaria (Won 1-0) v
                 Yugoslavia (Drew 2-2) v Czechoslovakia (Won 3-0) v
                 Portugal (Drew 0-0) 1975 v West Germany (Won 2-0) v
                 Cyprus (Won 1-0) v N.Ireland (Drew 0-0) v Wales
                 (Drew 2-2) v Scotland (won 5-1) v Switzerland (Won 2-
                 1) v Czechoslovakia (Lost 1-2) v Portugal (Drew 1-1)
                 1976 v Wales (Won 2-1) v Wales (Won 1-0) v N.Ireland
                 (Won 4-0) v Scotland (Lost 1-2) v Brazil (Lost 0-1) v
                 Finland (Won 4-1) v Republic of Ireland (Drew 1-1) v
                 Finland (Won 2-1) v Italy (Lost 0-2) 1977 v Holland
                 (Lost 0-2) v Luxembourg (Won 5-0) v Scotland (Lost 1-
                 2) v Brazil (Drew 0-0) v Argentina (Drew 1-1) v
                 Uruguay (Drew 0-0) v Switzerland (Drew 0-0) v
                 Luxembourg (won 2-0) v Italy (won 2-0) 1978 v West
                 Germany (Lost 1-2) v N.Ireland (Won 1-0) v Scotland
                 (Won 1-0) v Denmark (Won 4-3) v Republic of Ireland
                 (Drew 1-1) 1979 v N.Ireland (Won 4-0) v N.Ireland
                 (Won 2-0) v Scotland (Won 3-1) v Bulgaria (Won 3-0)
                 v Austria (Lost 3-4) v Denmark (Won 1-0) v Bulgaria
                 (Won 2-0) 1980 v Republic of Ireland (Won 2-0) v
                 Argentina (Won 3-1) v Wales (Lost 1-4) v Scotland
                 (Won 2-0) v Belgium (Drew 1-1) v Spain (Won 2-1) v
                 Romania (Lost 1-2) 1981 v Spain (Lost 1-2) v Brazil
                 (Lost 0-1) v Switzerland (Lost 1-2) v Hungary (Won 3-
                 1) v Norway (Lost 1-2) 1982 v N.Ireland (Won 4-0) v
                 Finland (won 4-1) v Luxembourg (Won 9-0) 1983 v
                 Luxembourg (Won 4-0)

Spotted by Scunthorpe United playing for the Skegness Youth Club, he had been associated with Notts County, playing one 'A' team game for the Meadow Lane club.

It was Bill Shankly who paid Scunthorpe £18,000 for the 19-year-old goalkeeper who had made just 50 senior appearances for the Irons in the lower divisions. Shankly's assessment of the man was that he was possibly the most important factor in Liverpool's continued success throughout the decade of the seventies. Indeed, in eleven seasons, Clemence missed a mere six league games, amassing over 650 appearances as Liverpool dominated British football.

After serving the almost mandatory lengthy stint in the Anfield reserves, he took over from Tommy Lawrence as the regular 'keeper.

Clemence immediately impressed with his safe handling and sharp reflexes. He got down quickly to low shots, knew when and when not to come off his line and had great positional sense. In his first full season, he conceded only 22 goals in 41 games, helping the Reds equal the First Division record of 24 in a season. In 1978-79 he went even better, only letting in 16 goals.

Of course, being behind one of the world's best defences, he needed to have great powers of concentration. He was kept idle for long periods, not getting a touch of the ball. It was a measure of his greatness that when he did have to respond, he would produce a top-class save. Of lightweight build and very athletic, he was able to spring several feet into the air and claim the ball with a very safe pair of hands. He was also one of the first goalkeepers to act as a sweeper behind his defence, leaving his penalty-area to cut out the long through ball. His world-class saves were many, but perhaps there were none more important than in the 1975-76 UEFA Cup away leg at Dynamo Dresden. He saved a penalty by diving full length to his right to reach a hard low shot and keep the tie goalless after ninety minutes.

One of the finest goalkeepers in the history of the game, he was unlucky to be around at the same time as Peter Shilton, for throughout his illustrious career at international level in which he won 61 caps, he was always vying for the Number One jersey with Shilts.

During his time with Liverpool, Clemence won five League Championship medals, three European Cup winners' medals, two UEFA Cup winners' medals, two FA Cup winners' medals and a League Cup and European Super Cup winners' medals. He was also on the losing side in two FA Cup Finals, one League Cup Final and one European Super Cup Final.

In August 1981 he announced that he was looking for a new challenge even though he was still at the top of his game and moved to Tottenham Hotspur for a fee of £300,000.

He made his Spurs' debut at Wembley in the 1981 Charity Shield and soon proved that at last the White Hart Lane club had a 'keeper to replace Pat Jennings. In that opening season with Spurs, he played his part in helping them retain the FA Cup and reach the League Cup Final where they lost to Liverpool. In his first six seasons at White Hart Lane, Clemence missed just 23 league games, most of those in 1983-84 when injury also meant that he by-passed the UEFA Cup success and again appeared in an FA Cup Final, picking up a losers' medal in 1987. Having completed 1,000 first-class games in 1985, Clemence was rewarded for his services to football with the MBE in the 1987 Birthday Honours list. After having sustained a serious knee injury in October 1987, he was forced to retire.

He was immediately appointed goalkeeping coach at Spurs, later being upgraded to assistant first-team coach at White Hart Lane. After a spell as manager of Barnet, Clemence became England's full-time goalkeeping coach.

ERNEST COLEMAN

Born	19 October 1889. Steyning, Sussex.
Died	15 June 1958.
Career	Croydon Amateurs; Dulwich Hamlet (1912 - 1925); also represented Surrey (1913) and London (1913 and 1920)
Internationals	1921 v Wales (Drew 0-0)

Ernest Coleman began his career with Croydon Amateurs before joining Dulwich Hamlet in 1912. After a series of outstanding displays in his first season with the club, he was chosen to represent both Surrey and London. He later won England amateur international honours and in 1920 won an FA Amateur Cup winners' medal.

The following year he was appointed captain of Dulwich Hamlet and won full international honours when he played against Wales at Ninian Park in March 1921. Despite having an outstanding game and keeping a clean sheet in a goalless draw, it was his only appearance at this level.

He continued to play for Dulwich Hamlet until 1925 when this colourful personality of the amateur game, retired to serve on the club's committee for a good number of years. An accountant by profession, he also acted as a selector and member of Dulwich Hamlet's finance committee. Later he became the club's Hon. Assistant Treasurer, retiring on health grounds in 1956, whereupon he was made a life member.

JOE CORRIGAN

Born	18 November 1948. Manchester.
Career	Sale FC; Manchester City (January 1967) Seattle Sounders (March 1983) Brighton and Hove Albion (September 1983) Norwich City on loan (September 1984) Stoke City on loan (October 1984) retired through injury February 1985.
Internationals	1976 v Italy (Won 3-2) 1978 v Brazil (Drew 1-1) 1979 v Wales (Drew 0-0) 1980 v N.Ireland (Drew 1-1) v Australia (Won 2-1) 1981 v Wales (Drew 0-0) v Scotland (Lost 0-1) 1982 v Wales (Won 1-0) v Iceland (Drew 1-1)

All Joe Corrigan had ever wanted to do since the age of four was to be a goalkeeper, so when he got the opportunity to go to Maine Road in 1966, he leapt at it, even though he came from the Red area of Manchester! After being singled out in the club trials where he gave some highly impressive performances, he turned professional in January 1967.

His first team debut for Manchester City was in the Football League Cup tie against Blackpool at Maine Road in October of the same year. The game ended all-square at 1-1 and though he had kept his side in the game with a number of important saves, he had to wait until March 1969 for his Football League debut at Portman Road, Ipswich beating City 2-1.

In his early days he was always in the shadow of Harry Dowd and Ken Mulhearn, though when he did get a chance he was inconsistent. Despite this unimpressive start to his league career, he fought hard to establish himself but faced another crisis of confidence when in 1975, City signed Keith MacRae for £100,000 from Motherwell. Out of favour with the then City manager Ron Saunders, he asked for a transfer and was transfer-listed

in February 1974. However, once again the 6ft 4 ins goalkeeper buckled down and won back his first team place, going on to serve City for a further nine years.

Manchester City have had three outstanding 'keepers since the war - Frank Swift, Bert Trautmann and Joe Corrigan was the third. I am sure that if he had been around at a different time than Ray Clemence and Peter Shilton, he would have collected far more than the nine international caps he did win. He won his first in 1976 coming on as a substitute against Italy in New York and his last against Iceland in 1982. He also played in an unofficial international for England against Athletico Bilbao in 1981, plus ten appearances for England 'B'.

His best season for City was 1976-77 when he only conceded 34 goals in his 42 appearances, keeping 22 clean sheets.

He won League Cup honours in 1970 and 1976 and a European Cup Winners' Cup medal in 1970 when City beat Gornik Zabrze 2-1. When City played Tottenham Hotspur at Wembley in the 1981 FA Cup Final, Corrigan had looked unbeatable - the game ending at 1-1. For his heroics between the posts, Corrigan was named man-of-the-match, though he was beaten three times in the replay as the White Hart Lane club won 3-2.

Corrigan played in 476 league games for Manchester City and in another 116 in Cup matches, making him second only to Alan Oakes in terms of the number of first-team appearances for City. In March 1983, City transferred him to Settle Sounders in the NASL for £30,000. He later returned to these shores to play for Brighton and Hove Albion, Norwich City and Stoke City before retiring.

Since then, he has coached goalkeepers at a number of clubs including Celtic, Middlesbrough, Tranmere Rovers and Barnsley before being offered a post at Anfield as Liverpool's first full-time goalkeeping coach.

D

TEDDY DAVISON

Born	2 September 1887. Gateshead.
Died	6 January 1971

Career	Gateshead St Chads; Sheffield Wednesday (April 1908) Mansfield Town as player-manager (June 1926) Chesterfield secretary/manager (December 1927) Sheffield United secretary/manager (June 1932) Chesterfield manager (August 1952 to May 1958 when he became the club's chief scout.
Internationals	1922 v Wales (Won 1-0)

In the record books as the smallest goalkeeper (5ft 7ins) to play for England, Teddy Davison has a special place in Sheffield football history, having played for Wednesday for 18 years and later managed United for 20 years.

Davison had ample courage and determination and made up for his lack of inches with a fine sense of anticipation and razor-sharp reflexes. Davison was especially adept at saving penalty kicks and on a number of occasions he saved two in a game. It was a penalty save in a trial game in 1908 which prompted Sheffield Wednesday to sign him.

He eventually replaced Jack Lyall in the Owls' goal and made 102 consecutive appearances for the club until 1913. Davison played eight times for the Sheffield FA and 13 times for the FA on their tour of Australia in 1925 but at club level the honours eluded him. A model of consistency, he was seldom heard to offer criticism or complaint but he was once so incensed by a goal 'scored' by Sheffield United's Joe Kitchen that he chased after the referee to complain. 'He put the ball in with his hand' said the Wednesday goalkeeper. If the referee didn't believe him, there were others that did and shortly afterwards he was sent a card addressed to 'George Washington, Owlerton'.

Davison, who played in 424 League and Cup games for Sheffield Wednesday, played for England against Wales in March 1922 at Anfield, winning his chance by making difficult saves look easy and using his strength to make brave, acrobatic saves.

After a spell as player-manager of non-League Mansfield Town, Davison moved to Chesterfield as the club's manager. In his second season at Saltergate he led the Spireites to the Third Division (North) Championship.

In June 1932 he received a lucrative offer to manage Sheffield United and in 1934 took them to the FA Cup Final where they gave the mighty Arsenal a run for their money before losing to a lone goal from Ted Drake. United went close to promotion in 1935-36 and 1937-38, in the latter season, missing out only on goal average. The following season though they were runners-up and returned to the First Division. After relegation in 1948-49, the Blades almost achieved an immediate return, losing out to Wednesday on goal average the following season ! In August 1952, Davison went back to Saltergate to manage Chesterfield where he developed a successful youth scheme, helping the club reach the FA Youth Cup Final. In goal was Gordon Banks, whom Davison helped to develop before selling him to Leicester City. Davison later became Chesterfield's scout, dying at the age of 83 in 1971 after having spent virtually the whole of his life in football.

JERRY DAWSON

Born	18 March 1888. Holme nr Burnley.
Died	8 August 1970
Career	Portsmouth Rovers (Todmorden) Holme FC, Cliviger FC Burnley (February 1907) retired 1929, later scouted for Burnley.
Internationals	1921 v Ireland (Drew 1-1) 1922 v Scotland (Lost 0-1)

Jeremiah Dawson was born in Holme-in-Cliviger just outside Burnley and first played football for nearby Portsmouth Rovers whilst serving an apprenticeship to the Cliviger village blacksmith. After a series of out-standing displays for the village football team, he came to the attention of Burnley for whom after a few games in the reserves, he signed professional forms.

He made his league debut for the Clarets in April 1907 as Stockport County were beaten 3-0 at Turf Moor. Soon after the start of the 1907-08 season, Burnley's regular 'keeper Billy Green was displaced and Jerry Dawson's monumental league career had begun in earnest. His consistency and sheer brilliance week after week was the foundation on which Burnley's success - promotion to the First Division in 1912-13 - was based.

His performances brought international recognition for the first time in February 1910 when he was chosen to represent the Football League against the Scottish League at Ewood Park. The following year, his display in the same fixture at Ibrox Park brought him a standing ovation by the partisan Scottish crowd !

During the club's FA Cup run of 1913-14, Dawson was approaching the peak of his ability. He had performed brilliantly in all of the club's matches up to the semi-final when in a goalless draw against Sheffield United at Old Trafford, he twisted a thigh muscle when collecting a high cross.

Four days later in the replay, Ronnie Sewell, the club's reserve 'keeper took his place as Tommy Boyle scored the goal that took the Clarets through to their first FA Cup Final. Sewell continued in goal for the club's next four league games but just one week before the final, Dawson returned to the side for the league game at Manchester City.

The Maine Road club won 4-1 in a game in which Dawson was again injured, this time suffering badly bruised ribs. The question was, would he be fit for the final ? On the Friday prior to the big game, Dawson met Burnley manager John Haworth in private and told him he had decided not to play.

Even though he felt fit, he thought it too much of a risk and he may not last the whole match. Sewell stepped up again and performed admirably as a goal by Bert Freeman gave Burnley a 1-0 win over Liverool.

Jerry Dawson's act of selflessness has gone down in football history and as a gesture of appreciation by the Clarets and the game's authorities, a special medal was struck in honour of the Burnley 'keeper.

In 1914-15, Dawson was back between the posts as the Clarets finished fourth in Division One and was still the club's first-choice 'keeper when league football resumed in 1919-20. Despite missing eight games in mid-season with a damaged shoulder, he was instrumental in the club finishing as runners-up in the top flight. When Burnley won the League Championship in 1920-21, Dawson was injured in the opening game of the season but was soon back in action, playing his part to the full.

The Burnley 'keeper's long-awaited England debut came in October 1921 when he played in a 1-1 draw against Ireland in Belfast. He won his other international cap against Scotland at Birmingham in April 1922, a match England lost 1-0.

After breaking Fred Barron's appearance record in December 1922, Dawson incredibly played another three full seasons as the club's first-choice 'keeper before deciding to retire. He made the last of his 569 League and Cup appearances against Liverpool on Christmas Day 1928 at the age of 40 years 282 days. He then joined the club's coaching staff whilst distinguishing himself as an accomplished batsman in the Lancashire League. A lifelong bachelor, Jerry Dawson was a dedicated professional, long-remembered in the town of Burnley.

TED DITCHBURN

Born	24 October 1921. Gillingham.
Career	Northfleet Paper Mills; Tottenham Hotspur amateur cs 1937 (sent to Spurs' nursery side, Northfleet FC for development 1938) turned professional cs 1939; Romford (April 1959) Brentwood (August 1965)
Internationals	1948 v Switzerland (Won 6-0) v Sweden (Lost 1-3) 1953 v United States (Won 6-3) 1956 v Wales (Won 3-1) v Yugoslavia (Won 3-0) v Denmark (Won 5-2)

The son of a professional boxer and an England Schools trialist, Ted Ditchburn played for Northfleet Paper Mills before joining the groundstaff of Tottenham Hotspur. On signing amateur forms, the Gillingham-born 'keeper was sent to Northfleet but with the outbreak of the Second World War, 'guested' for Dartford. Ditchburn's debut was in the Football League South in May 1940 against Norwich City but National Service meant he was only able to turn out occasionally for Spurs and played more games during the war as a 'guest' for Aberdeen and Birmingham City than he did for the White Hart Lane club.

However, the hostilities did give him an early taste of representative football as he represented both the Royal Air Force and the Football Association XI's as well as playing in two wartime internationals for England, the first against Scotland in February 1944.

When the war ended, Ditchburn returned to White Hart Lane and made his Football League debut for Spurs in the 2-1 home defeat by Birmingham City on the opening day of the 1946-47 season. During his first seven seasons in the Tottenham goal, Ted Ditchburn missed two League and Cup games and played in a club record 247 consecutive games.

Five appearances for the Football League were followed by his first full cap against Switzerland at Highbury in December 1948, a match England won 6-0. A member of England's World Cup squad in 1950, he won five more caps for his country and also played for England 'B' twice and the Football League once more.

Ditchburn was unfortunate to play in an era when England were well-served by top-class 'keepers such as Frank Swift and Bert Williams.

He was ever-present in the Second Division Championship winning team of 1949-50 and the League Championship winning side of the following season. Ditchburn was a magnificent catcher of crosses, breathtakingly agile on his line and endowed with great concentration. A particularly good ground shot-stopper and possessor of a mighty kick, his one weakness was his punching.

Ditchburn also had a quick accurate throw and in conjunction with full-back Alf Ramsey pioneered and perfected the art of starting attacks with the sort of early distribution from the back which was part and parcel of Spurs' 'Push and Run' style in the early 1950s.

After losing his place in the Spurs' side to Ron Reynolds for a brief spell, Ditchburn fought his way back to take his total of League and Cup appearances for the North London club to 453.

In fact his career was only ended by a broken finger sustained in the 4-2 defeat by Chelsea in August 1958 and eight months later - by now the only survivor from the 1950-51 Championship team - he became player-manager of non-League Romford.

In August 1965 he signed for Brentwood Town for whom he played a few games whilst building a successful sports outfitters business in Romford where he also owned a toys and games shop and had an interest in a printing business.

F

TIM FLOWERS

Born	3 February 1967. Kenilworth.
Career	Wolverhampton Wanderers (August 1984) Southampton (June 1986) Swindon Town on loan (March 1987 and November 1987) Blackburn Rovers (November 1993) Leicester City (July 1999)
Internationals	1993 v Brazil (Drew 1-1) 1994 v Greece (won 5-0) 1995 v Nigeria (Won 1-0) v Uruguay (Drew 0-0) v Japan (Won 2-1) v Sweden (Drew 3-3) v Brazil (Lost 1-3) 1996 v China (Won 3-0) 1997 v Italy (Won 2-0) 1998 v Switzerland (Drew 1-1) v Morocco (Won 1-0)

Tim Flowers began his career with Wolverhampton Wanderers, joining the Molineux staff as an apprentice in June 1983, turning professional in August 1984 after putting in some superb performances for the Youth and Central League teams. Capped by England for both the Youth and Under-21 teams, he was given his senior baptism for the Wanderers by manager Tommy Docherty on the opening day of the 1984-85 season, at home to Sheffield United in a Second Division game which finished 2-2. He went on to play in 38 league games that season but the club were relegated to the Third Division and in 1985-86, relegated yet again, this time to the Fourth Division.

Flowers had a loan spell at Southampton without playing a match for the Saints before eventually joining the south coast club on a permanent basis as Peter Shilton's understudy.

He made a less than auspicious start, conceding five goals on his First Division debut at Old Trafford. In his second game against Arsenal he fractured a cheekbone and had two loan spells at Swindon Town before finally breaking into the Southampton side on a regular basis.

After missing just four games between 1989-90 and 1991-92, he was everpresent in 1992-93, when he consistently presented a formidable barrier in the club's first season in the Premier League. He kept 12 clean sheets that

season, at the end of which he won his first England cap in a 1-1 draw against a good Brazilian side in the USA Cup match.

A good shot-stopper and possessing great concentration, he had played in 234 League and Cup games for the Saints when he was allowed to join Blackburn Rovers for £2.4 million in November 1993.

He showed supreme temperament when spending long spells under-employed during Rovers' Premier League Championship winning season of 1994-95, at the end of which he was one of six Blackburn players elected to the PFA Premier League 'Team of the Year'.

At his best, Flowers was a positive influence on the Blackburn team, a player who could inspire others but after a series of injuries including a torn bicep cost him a place in the Rovers' side, Flowers, who had appeared in 203 League and Cup games for the Ewood club, left to play for Leicester City.

WILLIE FOULKE

Born	12 April 1874. Dawley, Shropshire.
Died	1 May 1916

Career	Alfreton FC; Blackwell Colliery; Sheffield United cs 1894; Chelsea (May 1905) Bradford City (April 1906).
Internationals	1897 v Wales (Won 4-0)

Tipping the scales at over 24 stone, Willie Foulke was the largest man ever to play in the Football League.

As an infant William and his elder brother Thomas, were taken by their grandparents to the village of Blackwell in Derbyshire. Not surprisingly they both started their working lives in the colliery and it was here that Willie's footballing career began.

As goalkeeper of the successful Blackwell Colliery team, Foulke soon attracted the attention of the local professional clubs. Derby County appeared favourites to sign Foulke but while he thought over the move, Sheffield United moved in and won the battle for his signature after Willie's brother had advised him to join the Blades.

At Bramall Lane, Foulke joined a team of very talented players including Ernest Needham, who won 16 caps for England. Foulke made his debut for United on 1 September 1894 against West Bromwich Albion and quickly won over the Bramall Lane faithful. Although his first season with the

Yorkshire club was not a marked success, Foulke would win praise for his performances even when the side struggled.

In the two seasons that followed, Foulke's reputation and waistline grew! In 1896-97, United finished runners-up in the First Division, it was a campaign in which Willie won his only England cap. The following season the Blades won the League Championship and a year later won the FA Cup, beating Derby County 4-1. When Willie was presented with his medal by the Prime Minister Balfour, the giant goalkeeper informed him that he did not think he was the right man for the job - and who was Balfour to argue!

In 1901, Sheffield United lost 3-1 to Tottenham Hotspur of the Southern League in the FA Cup Final at Crystal Palace. Though the history books tell us the story of the only occasion that a non-League club has won the trophy, few tell of Willie's antics. It is reported that he ran virtually stark naked around the corridors of the Crystal Palace seeking revenge on the Tottenham players after the Blades were held to a 2-2 draw in the first meeting.

The following year, Sheffield United won the FA Cup for a second time, beating Southampton 2-1 after the first game had been drawn. Such was Foulke's performance in that game that the Sheffield MP, Sir Howard Vincent declared that 'surely Foulke is the greatest goalkeeper of all-time'.

Willie Foulke was United's first-choice 'keeper for ten years but towards the end of the 1904-05 season, it was clear his days at Bramall Lane were coming to an end.

Newly-formed Chelsea secured his services in the summer of 1905 and for much of the following season, he held the best defensive record in the Football League. However, his stay at Stamford Bridge was brief and in April 1906, Bradford City lured him back to Yorkshire.

Sadly, his career at Valley Parade was over in less than a year after a leg injury - which was aggravated by rheumatism - made it difficult for him to continue playing.

Foulke was also a keen cricketer and played four games for Derbyshire, one of his innings against Essex at Leyton bringing him considerable praise.

On retirement, Foulke continued to be involved in sport, firstly working as a seaside attraction in 'beat the goalie' on Blackpool beach and then as a referee in the Sheffield racing handicaps. Sadly, his health began to deteriorate and after a short spell in a nursing home, he died. His funeral at the Burngreave cemetery was attended by many of his former team-mates who came to pay tribute to a great character.

FRED FOX

| Born | 22 November 1898. Highworth nr Swindon. |
| Died | 15 May 1968 |

| Career | Swindon Town (cs 1914) Abertillery (cs 1919) Preston North End (cs 1921) Gillingham (July 1922) Millwall (May 1925) Halifax Town (June 1927) Brentford (March 1928) |
| Internationals | 1925 v France (Won 3-2) |

Fred Fox began his career with his home-town club, Swindon Town, playing for the Robins during the First World War. When the hostilities ceased he had a brief spell with Abertillery before joining Preston North End in the summer of 1921. He appeared in just three league games for the Lilywhites before leaving Deepdale after one season to play for Gillingham.

He made his debut for the Kent club at Brighton and Hove Albion in October 1922 where he gave a solid performance. Whilst with the Gills he became an international proposition. He was an outstanding goalkeeper with a safe pair of hands and keen anticipation. In May 1925 whilst still a Gillingham player, he became the first Third Division goalkeeper to be capped for England in the match against France in Paris, a game England won 3-2. By the time the match was played, Fox, who had appeared in 119 League and Cup games for Gillingham, had signed for Millwall for £650, though he hadn't turned out for the Lions by that time.

After two seasons at the Den, Fox went north to play for Halifax Town but after one season, he left The Shay to return to London and see out his first-class career with Brentford.

G

LESLIE GAY

Born	24 March 1871. Brighton.
Died	1 November 1949
Career	Brighton College (XI 1889) Cambridge University (Blue 1892) Old Brightonians and Corinthians 1891 to 1894.
Internationals	1893 v Scotland (Won 5-2) 1894 v Wales (Won 5-1) v Scotland (Drew 2-2)

After attending Brighton College, Leslie Gay went up to Cambridge University where in 1892 he won a Blue. The following year, this very skilled and quite fearless goalkeeper won the first of three full caps for England when he played in a 5-2 win over Scotland at Richmond in April 1893. By the time he made his second appearance for England just under a year later, Gay was playing for Old Brightonians. His best performance for England came at Hampden Park in April 1894 when he saved a number of goal-bound shots in a 2-2 draw against Scotland.

Gay was also a distinguished cricketer - a wicket-keeper and tail-end batsman. He enjoyed a brief county career which comprised four matches for Somerset, followed six years later in 1900 by nine appearances for Hampshire. Whilst touring Australia with Stoddart's team, he made his only Test appearance in the opening match of the series. Although he shared a ninth-wicket partnership of 73 with Lancashire's Johnny Briggs, he missed four catches plus a run out and was replaced by Hylton Philipson for the remainder of the series.

The double international was also a very good golfer, having represented Devon.

A land agent by profession, he had also worked as a coffee planter in Sri Lanka during the 1890s.

BILLY GEORGE

Born	29 June 1874. Shrewsbury.
Died	4 December 1933
Career	Woolwich Ramblers; Trowbridge Town; Aston Villa (October 1897) Birmingham as trainer (July 1911)
Internationals	1902 v Wales (Drew 0-0) v Ireland (Won 1-0) v Scotland (Drew 2-2)

Shrewsbury-born goalkeeper Billy George began his career with Woolwich Ramblers in 1894 before joining the Royal Artillery in February 1895, assisting Trowbridge Town when on leave. A regular soldier, George was given a trial by Aston Villa in a friendly against West Bromwich Albion and after giving a near faultless display, was signed immediately. This infringed FA rules and Villa were fined £50, whilst George, along with Mr Fred Rinder and George Ramsay was suspended for a month.

Eventually, Villa persuaded Billy George to leave the army and turn professional with them in October 1897 and he made his debut for them in a 1-1 draw against West Bromwich Albion at the Hawthorns. It was a most profitable move for both club and player, for George, who missed very few games over the next 13 seasons, soon became acknowledged as one of the finest goalkeepers in the country.

He helped Villa win the First Division Championship in 1898-99 and 1899-1900, being ever-present in the latter season and in 1905 won an FA Cup winners' medal as Villa beat Newcastle United 2-0 at the Crystal Palace.

His form led to him winning three full caps for England, the first against Wales at Wrexham in March 1902. George, who kept clean sheets in his first two appearances for his country, also had a good game in the 2-2 draw against Scotland, but it was his last appearance at this level.

He played the last of his 398 League and Cup games for Aston Villa in a 1-1 draw at Woolwich Arsenal in March 1911, after which he became a trainer with Birmingham. George, who was also a fine county cricketer, playing for Warwickshire, Wiltshire and Shropshire, stayed at St Andrew's until 1914 when he left to work in the Austin Motor Factory at Longbridge, a job he held until his death at the age of 59 in December 1933.

HAROLD GOUGH

Born	31 December 1890. Chesterfield.
Died	16 June 1970
Career	Spital Olympic; Castleford Town; Bradford Park Avenue cs 1910; Castleford Town (August 1911) Sheffield United (April 1913) Castleford Town (January 1925) Harrogate (October 1926) Oldham Athletic (February 1927) Bolton Wanderers (December 1927) Torquay United (June 1928)
Internationals	1921 v Scotland (Lost 0-3)

Chesterfield-born goalkeeper Harold Gough began his Football League career with Sheffield United after playing for a number of local clubs including Spital Olympic, Castleford Town and Bradford. He made his league debut for the Blades in a 4-1 defeat against Tottenham Hotspur in September 1913, going on to be United's first-choice 'keeper for seven seasons either side of the First World War.

He won the FA Cup with Sheffield United in 1915, keeping a clean sheet in a 3-0 win over Chelsea at Old Trafford.

In the summer of 1920 he toured South Africa with an FA party and in April 1921 he won his only England cap when he played in the 3-0 defeat by Scotland at Hampden Park. Gough, who went on to appear in 335 League and Cup games for Sheffield United earned the description of 'cool, collected and very tough'. He certainly had to be for in those days, forwards could legally bundle goalkeepers over the goal-line!

Harold Gough's speciality was in dealing with high shots and his bravery and daring were renowned. He actually left Bramall Lane in January 1925 through taking over, against club rules, a Castleford public house and was suspended from close season to December 1924.

On leaving Sheffield United, he played non-League football for Castleford Town (again) and Harrogate before Oldham Athletic paid £450 for his services in February 1927. Signed following the transfer of Welsh international Bert Gray to Manchester City, Gough proved an expensive investment as Athletic had Gray's replacement already on their books in the shape of Jack Hacking.

After just four appearances for the Boundary Park club, Gough joined Bolton Wanderers before moving to Torquay United where in 1930 he was forced to retire through injury.

H

JACK HACKING

Born	22 December 1897. Blackburn.
Died	31 May 1955
Career	Blackburn Co-op; Blackpool (December 1919) Fleetwood cs 1925; Oldham Athletic (May 1926) Manchester United (March 1934) Accrington Stanley as player-manager (May 1935) Barrow manager (May 1949)
Internationals	1928 v Ireland (Won 2-1) v Wales (Won 3-2) 1929 v Scotland (Lost 0-1)

A former grocer's assistant, Jack Hacking joined Blackpool after army service with the RGA during World War One. His potential was not realised at Bloomfield Road and after just 33 appearances in six years with the club, he moved to neighbouring Fleetwood. A brief and successful spell with the Lancashire Combination outfit ended with a move to Oldham Athletic in May 1926.

A worthy successor to such Latics' notables as Howard Matthews, Ted Taylor and Albert Gray, Hacking proved to be a consistent and able custodian who won three England caps and represented the Football League team on two occasions. After 223 League appearances for the Boundary Park club he made the short move to Manchester United in March 1934.

After a year at Old Trafford during which time his inspired goalkeeping helped Manchester United retain their Second Division status, Hacking moved on to Accrington Stanley. His finest performance for United came in the club's final game of the 1934-35 season at Millwall which United won 2-0 to ensure that it was Millwall and not the Reds who were relegated.

At Peel Park, Hacking became the club's player-manager. He could hardly have had a more unpleasant initiation into the realms of management. Consecutive defeats of 6-0, 3-0, 4-2 and 4-0 must have been a bitter disappointment to him, more so since he was in goal ! He retired as a player after 17 appearances in Stanley's goal but in an emergency included himself in the Reserves at right-back in February 1936 and gave a sound display, revealing no indication to use his hands !

Hacking made an immediate impact on the Peel Park club and raised them to their highest league position since 1927-28. However, after twelve months in charge he shocked the directors and fans when he declined the terms offered him for the 1936-37 season. Fortunately for Stanley he quickly reconsidered and decided to stay. His hard work could not compensate for the loss of good players and Accrington finished the 1937-38 and 1938-39 seasons bottom of the Third Division (North).

Ironically when League football was brought to a halt in 1939, Accrington Stanley were top of the table. The outbreak of the hostilities saw Hacking leave Peel Park because of his war work but he returned in 1944 and the following campaign led the club to the Third Division North (West Region) Championship. In May 1949 the directors decided that the club needed a change of direction and parted company with Hacking. Within days of his departure he was appointed secretary-manager of Barrow, where he remained until his death in 1955.

HARRY HARDY

| Born | 14 January 1895. Stockport. |
| Died | 17 February 1969 |

| Career | Alderley Edge FC; Stockport County (January 1920) Everton (October 1925) Bury (July 1929) |
| Internationals | 1924 v Belgium (Won 4-0) |

A product of the well-known local Ward Street Boys, Stockport-born Harry Hardy began his league career with his home-town club where he became one of County's most consistent performers in his five and a half seasons at Edgeley Park. Replacing Joseph Bird who had conceded eight goals in the opening two games of the 1920-21 season - Cardiff City (Home 2-5) and Fulham (Away 1-3) - Hardy made his debut in the return match at Cardiff but could do little to reverse the trend as County lost 3-0. However, he retained his place in the side and went on to make 170 consecutive league appearances for County from his debut. The reason he missed the next game came as a result of his selection for the Football League against the Irish League on 11 October 1924, the day County entertained Southampton.

In 1921-22 when the Edgeley Park club won the Third Division (North) Championship, Hardy kept 23 clean sheets.

A little over eight weeks after playing for the Football League, he made his one full international appearance against Belgium at the Hawthorns, a match which England won 4-0. Since then, he has remained in the record books throughout County's history as the only player to win an England cap whilst with Stockport.

In March 1925 he was selected for a Football League representative tour of Australia, thus missing the end of County's league season. Arriving back in London on 31 August, he was expected to return immediately and play against The Wednesday the same day which he duly did, but two months later, Hardy, who had appeared in 214 League and Cup games for County, was transferred to Everton for £2,350.

He was immediately drafted into the Goodison Park club's first team but conceded seven goals in his first two games - Arsenal (Away 1-4) and Manchester United (Home 1-3). Though he kept his place throughout the rest of that season, he only appeared in six games - none on the winning side - when Everton won the League Championship in 1927-28. At the end of that season, he was transferred to Bury, making 27 appearances for the Shakers before retiring. Harry Hardy was an accomplished oboist and spent thirteen years as a professional musician.

SAM HARDY

Born	26 August 1883. Newbold, Chesterfield.
Died	24 October 1966.
Career	Newbold White Star; Chesterfield Town (April 1903) Liverpool cs 1905; Aston Villa (May 1912) Nottingham Forest (August 1921)

Internationals   1907 v Ireland (Won 1-0) v Wales (Drew 1-1) v
Scotland (Drew 1-1) 1908 v Scotland (Drew 1-1) 1909
v Ireland (Won 4-0) v Wales (Won 2-0) v Scotland
(Won 2-0) v Hungary (Won 4-2) v Hungary (Won 8-2)
v Austria (won 8-1) 1910 v Ireland (Drew 1-1) v Wales
(Won 1-0) v Scotland (Lost 0-2) 1912 v Ireland (Won 6-
1) 1913 v Scotland (Won 1-0) 1914 v Ireland (Lost 0-3)
v Wales (Won 2-0) v Scotland (Lost 1-3) 1919 v Ireland
(Drew 1-1) 1920 v Wales (Lost 1-2) v Scotland (Won 5-
4)

Probably the most famous of all England's goalkeepers in the period 1905 to 1924, Sam Hardy was one of the first students of sophisticated angles and the geometry of goalkeeping and as film footage shows, a goal-keeper who would have been in the front rank of any era. Legend has it that his anticipation was so sharp, he rarely had to dive for the ball and saved more penalties than any other goalkeeper.

He was an amateur centre-forward with Newbold White Star before becoming a professional with his local club, Chesterfield in April 1903. In January 1905 he kept goal for Chesterfield against Liverpool and conceded six but the Anfield club's manager Tom Watson had no doubts about his ability and quickly signed the young 'keeper for a fee of £500. He made his league debut for the Reds in October 1905, taking over from the great Ned Doig and by the end of the season, Liverpool were League champions. Doig had played in the first eight games of the season, conceding 20 goals as Liverpool lost five of those matches. They hardly looked Championship contenders yet once Hardy was in position, they lost only five more games with Hardy conceding just 26 goals.

In 1907 he played for England in all three home internationals, going on to win 21 caps, a phenomenal total for those days, in an international career that spanned thirteen years. Fourteen of those caps were won while he was at Liverpool but in May 1912 after he had played in 239 League and Cup games, he was surprisingly sold to Aston Villa.

He made his debut in the opening game of the following season, keeping a clean sheet as Villa beat Chelsea 1-0. At the end of his first season at Villa Park, he won an FA Cup winners' medal as Villa beat Sunderland 1-0 at Crystal Palace. In fact, in the six cup matches that season, Hardy only conceded one goal and that was in the 3-1 first round win at Derby County.

Also that season, he gained the first of another seven caps he was to win with England, starring in the 1-0 win over Scotland at Stamford Bridge.

During the First World War he served in the Royal Navy but 'guested' for Nottingham Forest when they won the Victory Shield in 1919. He returned to Villa for the start of the new league season at the end of which he won his second FA Cup winners' medal as the Villa Park club beat Huddersfield Town 1-0. He had played in 183 games for Aston Villa when in August 1921 he was allowed to join Nottingham Forest for his highest transfer fee of £1,000. Despite conceding four goals on his debut at Crystal Palace, it proved to be money well spent.

The great goalkeeper although aged 38, clearly had much to do with Forest winning the Second Division Championship in 1921-22 when the City Ground club conceded only 30 goals in 42 games, a record for the division. He played in 109 League and Cup games for Forest, keeping 41 clean sheets before an injury sustained against Newcastle United on 4 October 1924 forced him to retire at the age of 41. He then became a hotelier in Chesterfield.

JOHN HAWTREY

Born	19 July 1850. Eton, Bucks.
Died	17 August 1925.

Career	Old Etonians; Remnants; Also represented London and Berks and Bucks FAs.
Internationals	1881 v Wales (Lost 0-1) v Scotland (Lost 1-6)

John Hawtrey attended Eton College until 1864 and then Clifton College but did not play football at either educational establishment. On leaving school, he taught for several years at his father's school, Aldin House in Slough.

He began to play football for Old Etonians and in 1879 won an FA Cup winners' medal as they beat Clapham Rovers 1-0 in the final. Two years later whilst playing for London against Birmingham, he had such an outstanding game that he was chosen to represent England against Wales at Blackburn in March 1881. Two weeks later he was in goal when England were beaten 6-1 by Scotland at Kennington Oval. In a one-sided game, his goal was nearly always under siege as the Scots ran amok but match reports of the time say the visitors could have had many more goals if Hawtrey had not produced a number of outstanding saves.

As a goalkeeper, Hawtrey, who later played for Remnants, Berks and Bucks, was described as inconsistent, though when on his game, he was apparently brilliant. When his younger brother Charles found fame as an actor, John Hawtrey hung up his boots and followed him on to the stage, becoming a playwright under the name of John Trent-Hay. In later life, Hawtrey ran the journal 'Sporting World'.

HARRY HIBBS

Born	27 May 1906. Wilnecote, Staffs.
Died	23 April 1984.
Career	Wilnecote Holy Trinity; Tamworth Castle; Birmingham (May 1924) Walsall manager (August 1944 to June 1951) was permit player for de Havilands February 1953; Manager of Ware Town in the Delphian League (August 1960)
Internationals	1929 v Wales (Won 6-0) 1930 v Scotland (Won 5-2) v Germany (Drew 3-3) v Austria (Drew 0-0) v Ireland (Won 5-1) v Wales (Won 4-0) 1931 v Scotland (Lost 0-2) v Ireland (Won 6-2) v Wales (Won 3-1) v Spain (Won 7-1) 1932 v Ireland (Won 1-0) v Wales (Drew 0-0) v Austria (Won 4-3) 1933 v Scotland (Lost 1-2) v Italy (Drew 1-1) v Switzerland (Won 4-0) v Ireland (Won 3-0) v Wales (Lost 1-2) v France (Won 4-1) 1934 v Wales (Won 4-0) 1935 v Ireland (Won 2-1) v Scotland (Lost 0-2) v Holland (Won 1-0) v Germany (Won 3-0) 1936 v Wales (Lost 1-2)

England's number one goalkeeper between the wars, Harry Hibbs began his career as a centre-forward, leading the attack for Wilnecote Youths. He later switched to a goalkeeping role as a 17-year-old with Tamworth Castle in the Birmingham and District League.

Two years later, Birmingham were sufficiently impressed with his progress to offer him a full-time professional contract and on the final day of the

1925-26 season, he made his league debut for the Blues against Arsenal at Highbury. It was not the best of starts for the young 'keeper for two goals from Jimmy Brain and another from Tom Parker gave the Gunners a comfortable 3-0 victory. Hibbs fared even worse on his one appearance the following season when Tottenham Hotspur romped to a 6-1 win.

Whilst serving his apprenticeship in Birmingham's Reserve side, Hibbs developed the extraordinary powers of anticipation that enabled him to get his body behind even the hardest shots from the most acute angles. Although Harry Hibbs was only 5ft 9ins, this proved no handicap for he was rarely beaten in the air and dealt with low shots with equal facility.

During the early part of the 1929-30 season, Hibbs took over from Dan Tremelling in Birmingham's first team. He made 33 appearances that campaign, his performances earning him an international trial. In November 1930 he was selected for England against Wales at Stamford Bridge, a game in which Middlesbrough's George Camsell scored a hat-trick in England's 6-0 win.

Between his first cap and his last against Wales at Molineux in 1936, England played 33 internationals and Harry Hibbs was the selectors' first choice in 25 of those matches. During that spell he was on the losing side five times, three of them against Scotland at Hampden Park. He conceded only 26 goals in those matches, keeping a clean sheet on ten occasions.

Hibbs was on the losing side in the 1931 FA Cup Final when his opposite number in the West Bromwich Albion goal was his cousin Harold Pearson who had taken his place in the Tamworth Castle goal when Hibbs moved to St Andrew's.

In his 15 seasons with Birmingham, Harry Hibbs missed four matches through injury, until the 1938-39 season when he was still out of the side from October to April and managed only 13 appearances. Hibbs' last appearance for the Blues was his wartime benefit match against Aston Villa at St Andrew's on 13 April 1940 when Birmingham won 2-1.

As well as appearing for England, Hibbs played three times for the Football League against the Scottish League and in an unofficial international against South Africa in 1929.

In August 1944, Harry Hibbs was appointed manager of Walsall. He left Fellows Park in June 1951 and from February 1953 to May 1954, he turned out for de Havilands FC in Birmingham. He returned to the game as manager of Ware Town in the summer of 1960 and later had a brief spell in charge of Welwyn Garden City FC.

JACK HILLMAN

Born	1 May 1871. Tavistock.
Died	1 August 1955.
Career	Burnley (August 1891) Everton (February 1895) Dundee (June 1896) Burnley (March 1898) Manchester City (January 1902) Millwall Athletic (January 1907); Burnley trainer 1921-22.
Internationals	1899 v Ireland (Won 13-2)

One of the game's greatest characters, Jack Hillman was born in Tavistock, Devon in 1871 but his family moved to Burnley when he was a child. He was spotted playing junior football and after working his way up through the Clarets' ranks, made his first team debut in place of Archibald Kaye in a 1-0 defeat at Accrington on the opening day of the 1891-92 season, a campaign in which he was ever-present.

Hillman was second only to the huge Sheffield United 'keeper Billy Foulke in stature, standing over 6 feet tall and weighing 16 stone. After four seasons with the Clarets, he joined Everton, playing in 38 games before signing for Dundee. His stay in Scotland was brief and in March 1898 he returned to Turf Moor.

Known as 'The Burly One' his form attracted the attention of the England selectors and the following season he made his international debut in a 13-2 win over Ireland at Roker Park.

Burnley played their last league game of the 1899-1900 season at Nottingham Forest, needing a win to save them from relegation to Division Two. Unfortunately, they were beaten 4-0. The 'Athletic News' report said 'Burnley thoroughly deserved the beating they received' and that 'goalkeeper Hillman was in no way to blame'.

Jack Hillman was Burnley's skipper at the time and after the match, Forest alleged that he had told their captain. 'Look here, take this match easy today and we stand you £2 a man.' The complaint was lodged by letter to the FA. Forest's captain John McPherson was said to have replied 'No, it is more than I dare do and we are paid to play and go straight' to which Hillman responded 'All right I will see you at half-time.' After the interval, Burnley were two goals down and during the break Hillman was again alleged to have increased the bribe to £5 per man. McPherson replied 'No, if you want to do anything of that sort, you better see our committee.' Hillman admitted that the text of the complaint was true but that he did not know-ingly and with intent make an offer to the Forest team to take it easy. He maintained that this conversation was all chaff and arose out of an episode two weeks previously in which some suspicion had been thrown on the Forest side after losing 8-0 at West Bromwich Albion, a side they had earlier beaten 6-1. Hillman was suspended for the whole of the 1900-01 season.

He moved to Manchester City in 1902 where he won a Second Division Championship medal in 1903 and an FA Cup winners' medal in 1904. He ended his playing days with Millwall in 1907 before returning to Turf Moor yet again where he became reserve-team trainer, then first team trainer, continuing his association with the club into the mid 1920s.

ALAN HODGKINSON

Born   16 August 1936. Laughton, Rotherham.

Career   Thurcroft Youth Club, Worksop Town; Sheffield
      United (August 1954) Sheffield United assistant
      coach (January 1971) Gillingham assistant-manager
      (June 1975) subsequent coaching appointments have
      included Birmingham City (1981) Coventry City
      (1981) and Scotland (1986)

Internationals 1957 v Scotland (Won 2-1) v Republic of Ireland
      (Won 5-1) v Denmark (Won 4-1) v Republic of
      Ireland (Drew 1-1) 1960 v Wales (Won 5-1)

Alan Hodgkinson was 16 and playing for Worksop Town in the Midland League when Sheffield United manager Ray Freeman made his first approach. He wasn't the first manager to pretend that he was interested in another player when he made that contact and no doubt asked that perhaps Worksop might allow the young 'keeper to show his paces in United's Central League side.

The Blades were well aware of his ability and promise and that was confirmed in four Central League appearances at the end of the 1952-53 season. Three months after his last appearance for the reserves against Newcastle United, he signed professional forms for the Bramall Lane club.

United had just won the Second Division Championship and the goalkeeper of the time was Ted Burgin, known to the Blades' supporters as 'The Cat'. Although he was never awarded a full England cap, Burgin was chosen for the England 'B' team, was an England reserve and went on the FA tour of Australia. Ted Burgin taught Hodgkinson much of the arts and crafts of goalkeeping, often during the many afternoons they returned for extra training together on the old bowling green or in the gym.

Hodgkinson was given his first senior game in April 1954 at Bramall Lane in a floodlit game against Clyde and his Football League debut came at the end of August at Newcastle United.

Over the next two years, Hodgkinson learned a great deal playing for the Army while completing his National Service. They had a fairly useful side with players of the calibre of Bobby Charlton, Duncan Edwards, Cliff Jones and Dave Mackay in the team !

Probably the 1956-57 season was the most remarkable of Hodgkinson's 17 campaigns with the club. He still had five months to serve in the Army and had spent much of the previous season in the Blades' 'A' team when he was able to get leave. In September 1956 he made his first appearance in the England Under-23 side and was chosen for the match against France when Doncaster Rovers' Alick Jeffrey broke his leg.

On Christmas Day 1956 he made his first appearance in the United team for more than a year and injured his hand on the hard ground but after missing three games, he returned to first team action. The campaign ended with an appearance for the Football League against the Scottish League and his first full cap in a 2-1 win against Scotland at Wembley.

Hodgkinson remained in the England side for a run of four matches and was in contention for an England place for several years, being recalled to the national team to play Wales in 1960. In 1962 he also travelled to Chile with England's World Cup squad as reserve goalkeeper.

For Sheffield United in the period between August 1957 and May 1970 he missed just 26 league games ! Only Joe Shaw, who played in 631 league games for the Blades made more appearances than Alan Hodgkinson, who appeared in 576, the United 'keeper playing in 675 first team games.

Towards the end of his playing career, Hodgkinson was rewarded with a Lord Mayor's civic dinner and testimonial match.

One of Britain's most respected goalkeeping coaches, he now coaches custodians all over the British Isles including the Scottish national team, though at Bramall Lane, he always be remembered for his dependability, judgement and possessing one of the safest pair of hands in the game.

HARRY HOLDCROFT

Born	23 January 1909. Stoke-on-Trent.
Died	17 April 1983.
Career	Biddulph FC; Norten Druids; Whitfield Colliery; Port Vale (September 1926) Darlington (August 1928) Everton (August 1931) Preston North End (December 1932) Barnsley (1945) He later assisted Leyland Motors, Morecambe and Chorley.
Internationals	1936 V Wales (Lost 1-2) v Ireland (Won 3-1)

Born in the Potteries, Harry Holdcroft played for Biddulph, Norten Druids and Whitfield Colliery before joining Port Vale as an amateur in August 1926. He signed as a professional the following month and made his debut in a goalless home draw against Hull City in February 1927. However, he was unable to gain a regular place in the team and was quickly snapped up by Darlington where he stayed for three seasons before being transferred to Everton as reserve cover.

In December 1932, the Preston North End management team produced a brilliant stroke by signing both Holdcroft and hard-tackling full-back Harold Lowe for a bargain price from the Goodison club.

He made his debut for the Lilywhites in a 1-0 defeat at Southampton on Christmas Eve 1932, going on to play in 172 consecutive League and Cup games following his debut. In his first full season he helped North End win promotion to the First Division with a series of outstanding displays between the posts.

His skill, composure, agility and masterly handling, especially in the air, earned him the right to be named alongside the best 'keepers the club ever had - James Trainer and Peter McBride, Welsh and Scottish internationals respectively.

Ironically, the first time Holdcroft was missing from the North End line-up was due to the fact that he was playing for England against Wales on 17 September 1936. He also played against Ireland the following month, a match England won 3-1.

That same season, Preston North End reached the semi-final of the FA Cup but the week before the game, Holdcroft broke a finger in the game against Middlesbrough and so missed the semi-final and also the final itself against Sunderland.

The following season, North End returned to Wembley and defeated Huddersfield Town 1-0 in the final - in goal was Harry Holdcroft, keeping yet another clean sheet.

After 289 League and Cup games, 'Handsome Harry' as he was known, found his life interrupted by the Second World War, just as he was in his prime. Although he played occasionally during the war, 'guesting' for Burnley, Oldham Athletic and Manchester United amongst others, his North End career was at an end.

He later signed for Barnsley before playing local non-League football with Morecambe, Chorley and Leyland Motors.

EDDIE HOPKINSON

Born   29 October 1935. Wheatley Hill, Co Durham.

Career   Oldham Athletic cs 1951; Bolton Wanderers
                    (November 1952) retired in 1970 and joined
                    Bolton's coaching staff. Stockport County
                    assistant-manager (1975)

Internationals   1957 v Wales (Won 4-0) v N.Ireland (Lost 2-3)
                    v France (Won 4-0) 1958 v Scotland (Won 4-0)
                    v Portugal (Won 2-1) v Yugoslavia (Lost 0-5)
                    1959 v Scotland (Won 1-0) v Italy (Drew 2-2)
                    v Brazil (Lost 0-2) v Peru (Lost 1-4) v Mexico
                    (Lost 1-2) v United States (Won 8-1) v Wales
                    (Drew 1-1) v Sweden (Lost 2-3)

Born in Wheatley Hill, County Durham, Eddie Hopkinson became a naturalised Lancastrian when his family moved south to Royton near Oldham. He soon signed as an amateur for Oldham Athletic and was only 16 years of age when he played in three Third Division (North) games in 1951-52.

In the summer months he played cricket for Royton in the Central Lancashire League and until football stopped him, he was a county water-polo player.

At the end of the 1951-52 season, Oldham Athletic overlooked him, much to Bolton Wanderers' lasting satisfaction. He joined the Wanderers in August 1952, signing professional forms the following November. He played little football for Bolton during his National Service as he was stationed in Scotland.

His meteoric rise began in August 1956 when Bolton's regular goalkeeper Ken Grieves, the Lancashire cricketer, couldn't be released from his cricketing duties as the Red Rose county were chasing Championship honours. Eddie got his chance in the senior side against Blackpool and went through a brilliant first season without missing a game.

At 5ft 9 ins, he was one of the smallest goalkeepers in the First Division. In the summer of 1957 he was awarded the first of six England Under-23 caps on a tour behind the Iron Curtain. In October of that year he made his first full international appearance against Northern Ireland, going on to play against all three countries in the Home Internationals and eventually

against all three countries in the Home Internationals and eventually collecting 14 caps.

In 1958 he kept a clean sheet to win an FA Cup winners' medal as Bolton Wanderers beat Manchester United 2-0 at Wembley. At Norwich City in January 1969, he broke Bolton's long-standing appearance record set by Alex Finney. Eddie played in 578 matches for Bolton Wanderers and but for an injury which kept him out of the side for most of the 1958-59 season and another which put him out of action for a ten-match spell in the 1963-64 season, he would have passed the Finney record much earlier.

Professionals reckon that consistency is the true test of a top-class player and there were certainly few to rival Eddie Hopkinson in this aspect of his game.

He remained Bolton's first-choice goalkeeper until the middle of the 1969-70 season when injury forced his retirement. He was awarded a testimonial in May 1971 at Burnden Park, a game in which Portuguese World Cup stars Eusebio and Simoes played.

He became assistant-trainer at Burnden Park, coaching both the Youth and Reserve sides. He left in July 1974 to join nearby Stockport County as assistant-manager, his son Paul keeping goal for the Edgeley Park club.

He made an unexpected comeback when he volunteered to keep goal for the team he managed, Ashton United, when four players failed to turn up for the Cheshire League game at Witton. Witton won 7-0 but 'Hoppy' got a great ovation as he retired at half-time to make way for latecomers.

In 1979 he returned to his beloved Bolton as goalkeeping coach but eventually left the game to become a representative for a chemical company. He now works as a customer relations officer for Warburton Bakeries.

TED HUFTON

Born	25 November 1892. Southwell, Notts.
Died	2 February 1967.
Career	Atlas and Norfolk Works (Sheffield); Sheffield United cs 1912; West Ham United cs 1919; Watford (June 1932)
Internationals	1923 v Belgium (Drew 2-2) 1927 v Ireland (Lost 0-2) 1928 v Scotland (Lost 1-5) 1929 v Belgium (Won 5-1) v Spain (Lost 3-4) v France (Won 4-1)

Ted Hufton was signed by Sheffield United from local works side Atlas and Norfolk in 1912. He soon established himself in the Blades' first team but a broken nose in a trial game at the start of the 1914-15 season put him out of action and he lost his place in the United team that reached that season's FA Cup Final. Meanwhile, Hufton had joined the Coldstream Guards and was wounded in action in France. Whilst he was recuperating, he 'guested' for West Ham United and in 1919 he signed for the Upton Park club on a permanent basis for a fee of £350.

He made his debut for the Hammers in their first-ever Football League match on 30 August 1919, helping the club secure a point in a 1-1 home draw against Lincoln City. He helped the club to the first Wembley Cup Final where they lost 2-0 to Bolton Wanderers and to promotion to the First Division in 1922-23 when his outstanding performance in the game at Sheffield Wednesday two days after the final, gave the Hammers a 2-0 win.

That victory put the club back on top of the Second Division on goal average with Notts County and Leicester City who were also on 51 points. On the final Saturday of the season, all three teams were vying for the two promotion places but while Leicester were at lowly Bury, the Hammers met rivals Notts County at Upton Park. To the Hammers' surprise, Leicester lost 1-0 at Gigg Lane and though Notts County won by a similar margin, the East London club were promoted to the top flight for the first time in their history on goal average with Hufton having had an outstanding season.

This form led to him winning the first of six full caps for England when he played against Belgium in Antwerp, a match England drew 2-2. He broke his arm in one of his appearances for his country and but for this, he would surely have won more caps. As it was, between winning his first cap and his last in 1929, Hufton made more appearances for England than any of the other fifteen goalkeepers tried.

Hufton had a reputation for saving penalties and in a two-season spell, he saved 11 of the 18 spot-kicks he faced. He went on to play in 401 first team games for the Hammers before losing his place to George Watson. Granted a free transfer at the end of the 1932-33 season, he left Upton Park to play for Watford.

After the Second World War, the highly popular Hufton returned to Upton Park to work as a press steward. On leaving the playing arena, he worked in the motor trade. Accidents in January 1963 when knocked down by a motor scooter and a few months later by a car, marred his last years.

J

DAVID JAMES

Born	1 August 1970. Welwyn Garden City.
Career	Watford (July 1988) Liverpool (July 1992) Aston Villa (June 1999)
Internationals	1997 v Mexico (Won 2-0)

David James began his career with Watford where he spent two years in the shadow of Tony Coton but when the latter moved to Manchester City in the 1990 close season, he got the break that he had been looking for. He made his Football League debut at home to Millwall in August 1990 and except for one Zenith Data Systems Cup game, he was ever-present.

His form was so outstanding that he was soon called up to the England Under-21 squad and was regular first-choice throughout the season. During 1991-92, he turned out in all but three league games, conceding just 42 goals in 43 appearances and playing a large part in Watford's recovery from a relegation position to mid-table security. His name was constantly linked with Liverpool and other top flight clubs throughout the season and his eventual departure to Anfield in the summer of 1992 was hardly unexpected.

He made his league debut for the Reds on the opening day of the 1992-93 season, putting on a good display in a 1-0 defeat. However, the season as a whole was disappointing as he lost his place three times and showed a great deal of uncertainty in dealing with crosses and corners. In the match against Norwich City, a moment of sheer madness proved most costly. After collecting a corner, he mindlessly kicked John Polston and was shown the red card, having already received a yellow for up-ending Chris Sutton outside his area in the first-half. Norwich duly obliged with the only goal of the game from the spot when David Phillips beat the substitute 'keeper. Another disastrous display at Oldham Athletic a few days later prompted the recall of Bruce Grobbelaar for the final game of the season.

However, the following campaign saw James make the Liverpool Number One jersey his own. A goalkeeper somewhat in the mould of Bruce Grobbelaar, he began to display the ability to produce saves of world-class with his spectacular athleticism. Naturally flamboyant he was keen to replace Grobbelaar in the affections of the Reds' supporters by emulating his eccentricities, though he curbed his natural instincts to rush off his line to deal with every high cross into the penalty area and by so doing, became safer and more consistent. An honest professional, he blamed his moments of madness on a love of personal computer games !

Ever-present in 1994-95, he won England 'B' honours when coming on for Kevin Pressman against the Republic of Ireland in December 1995. Ever-present for the second consecutive season in 1995-96, James' form was recognised by his fellow professionals when selected for the PFA award-winning Premier League side.

His good form for Liverpool was finally recognised at full international level when selected by England for the match against Mexico when he kept a clean sheet in a 2-0 win.

James, who lost his place to Brad Friedel during the 1997-98 season, returned to first team action the following season but after a campaign in which Liverpool supporters saw both sides of his enigmatic character, James signed for Aston Villa for a fee of £1.7 million.

His performances helped Villa reach the FA Cup Final where they lost 1-0 to Chelsea. He was also selected by Kevin Keegan for the 28-man party prior to the European Championships but didn't make the final 22.

K

MATTHEW KINGSLEY

Born	15 November 1875. Turton nr Bolton.
Died	27 March 1960.
Career	Edgworth; Turton FC; Darwen cs 1896; Newcastle United (April 1898) West Ham United (May 1904) Queen's Park Rangers cs 1905; Rochdale (October 1907) Barrow cs 1908
Internationals	1901 v Wales (Won 6-0)

Somewhat hefty at 14 stone 4 lbs, Matt Kingsley played his early football for local sides Edgworth, Turton and Darwen before joining Newcastle United in April 1898. He took over the custodian's role during 1898-99, the Magpies' first in Division One, making his debut against Wolverhampton Wanderers.

He was noted for his fisted clearances in the style of the day and also had the unusual habit of constantly swinging his arms to and fro as he waited for the action.

After appearing in an international trial match, Kingsley became Newcastle United's first capped England player when he played against Wales at St James Park in 1901. For the record, England won 6-0 with Steve Bloomer scoring four of the goals. Kingsley was Newcastle's first-choice 'keeper for six seasons until Jimmy Lawrence arrived on the scene. An unusual character, who once scored two goals when playing as a goalkeeper in a friendly, he played in 189 games for the Magpies before leaving to play for West Ham United in May 1904.

After just one season at Upton Park, he joined Queen's Park Rangers where he again played for one campaign before deciding to retire. A year later he returned to the game to play for Rochdale before ending his career with Barrow.

Noted as the country's most reliable goalkeeper at the turn of the century, Kingsley later resided in the Blackburn area.

L

HARRY LINACRE

Born	20 June 1880. Aston-on-Trent, Derbyshire.
Died	11 May 1957.

Career	Aston-on-Trent FC; Draycott Mills; Derby County
	(December 1898) Nottingham Forest (August 1899)
Internationals	1905 v Wales (Won 3-1) v Scotland (Won 1-0)

Harry Linacre was the brother-in-law of Nottingham Forest and England internationals Frank and Fred Forman and like them, he was born in the Derbyshire village of Aston-on-Trent in 1880. Linacre attended and played for Loughborough Grammar School, before having spells with Aston-on-Trent and Draycott Mills.

His displays for the latter club attracted the attention of a number of top league sides and in December 1898 he joined Derby County. He had appeared in just two league games for the Rams when in August 1899 he left the Baseball Ground on the recommendation of Frank Forman and joined Nottingham Forest.

Making his league debut for Forest in a 2-2 draw at home to Bury on 4 November 1899, Linacre went on to prove an outstanding replacement for Dennis Allsop, the club's veteran goalkeeper. In his first full season, he was ever-present and only conceded 36 goals in his 34 appearances as Forest finished fourth in Division One. Linacre, who was also ever-present in 1903-04 and 1905-06 missed very few games for Forest in the nine seasons following his debut.

A firm favourite with the Forest fans, his consistency between the posts was rewarded with two England caps both in 1905, against Wales at Anfield (Won 3-1) and Scotland at Crystal Palace (Won 1-0).

He won a Second Division Championship medal in 1907 and also played for the Football League. In 1908-09, his last season with the club, he often seemed to be the only thing standing between Forest and defeat. He played the last of his 335 League and Cup games for Forest against the same opposition as he'd faced on his on his debut but unfortunately this time Bury won 2-0.

He left the club in the close season of 1909 and not surprisingly two seasons later, Forest were relegated.

On retirement, Linacre, a goalkeeper who was advantaged by a long reach and instinctive reflex actions, was in business with Frank Forman in a building contractors firm.

M

COLIN McDONALD

Born	15 October 1930. Summerseat nr Bury.
Career	Hawkshaw St Mary's; Burnley amateur (August 1948) part-time professional (October 1948) Headington United on loan in 1950-51; Burnley (July 1952) Wycombe Wanderers coach (August 1961) Bury chief scout (October 1961) Altrincham as a player (January 1965) Bury chief scout (May 1967) Bolton Wanderers chief scout (October 1968) Bury administrative manager (August 1969) general manager (May 1970) subsequently youth coaching posts with Oldham Athletic and Tranmere Rovers.
Internationals	1958 v Soviet Union (Drew 1-1) v Soviet Union (Drew 2-2) v Brazil (Drew 0-0) v Austria (Drew 2-2) v Soviet Union (Lost 0-1) v N.Ireland (Drew 3-3) v Soviet Union (Won 5-0) v Wales (Drew 2-2)

Colin McDonald's father had played football as a professional and was also a goalkeeper but it was Jack Marshall, then a full-back on Burnley's books who recognised the tremendous potential of the teenage 'keeper. Marshall arranged with Burnley manager Cliff Britton for the young McDonald to be given a trial at Turf Moor and it wasn't too long after that when he signed for the Clarets as an an amateur in 1948. He was still following his trade as a plumber when he was taken on as a part-time professional on his eighteenth birthday.

McDonald had made his Central League debut for the Clarets in May 1950 but then whilst on National Service, had a spell on loan with Headington United (later to become Oxford United) of the Southern League. Despite them beating Wycombe Wanderers in the FA Cup, the Manor Ground club were thrown out of the competition because of McDonald's apparent ineligibility to play for the club in the FA Cup !

On his return to Turf Moor, he signed as a full-time professional in July 1952 but had to wait until April 1954 before making his league debut in a First Division match at Aston Villa. Though the Clarets lost 5-1 that day, Colin McDonald was in the side to stay.

In fact, he hardly missed a game from then on in a virtual succession of faultless performances behind a Burnley team that was slowly building towards success at the turn of the decade. Despite suffering a broken ankle in the match at Chelsea in December 1956, allowing Adam Blacklaw a chance of first team football, McDonald only missed eight games.

Inevitably his performances attracted the attention of the International selectors and in March 1958, he played for the Football League in a 4-1 win over the Scottish League at Newcastle's St James Park.

McDonald, who was selected for the England squad for the 1958 World Cup Finals in Sweden, made his full international debut in a friendly match against the Soviet Union in the Lenin Stadium in Moscow, a game England drew 1-1. McDonald played in all four of England's World Cup games including giving an outstanding display of goalkeeping in the goalless draw against the eventual world champions, Brazil in Gothenburg. It was a performance that went a long way in helping him being voted the best 'keeper in the tournament.

During the following season, there were three more appearances for England and another Football League representative game but on 17 March 1959, tragedy struck. Whilst playing for the Football League against the League of Ireland in Dublin, McDonald broke his leg and though no-one knew it at the time, he never played first-class football again.

During the Clarets' League Championship winning season of 1959-60 McDonald played for the club's junior and Central League team but in the summer of 1961, he had to accept that his career was over.

After leaving Turf Moor, he coached Wycombe Wanderers before acting as chief scout first for Bury and then Bolton Wanderers. He rejoined Bury as General Manager before acting as team manager for a three-month spell. Later he coached Oldham Athletic and Tranmere Rovers before ending his involvement with the game.

Possibly Burnley's greatest-ever 'keeper, Colin McDonald was at his peak when the injury cruelly cut short a brilliant career.

ALBERT McINROY

Born	23 April 1901. Walton-le-Dale nr Preston.
Died	7 January 1985.
Career	Upper Walton cs 1919; Coppull Central cs 1920 Preston North End 1921-22; High Walton 1922; Leyland Motors 1922; Sunderland (May 1923) Newcastle United (October 1929) Sunderland (June 1934) Leeds United (May 1935) Gateshead (June 1937)
Internationals	1926 v Ireland (Drew 3-3)

At St Thomas' High School, Preston, Albert McInroy was an outside-left but after leaving school and getting a job as a packer at the Preston Co-operative Society, he played in goal for local sides Upper Walton and Coppull Central. He signed amateur forms with Preston North End at the start of the 1921-22 season but after a few reserve games, he left to play for High Walton United before joining Leyland Motors in November 1922.

After some impressive performances, he signed for Sunderland in May 1923 and was given his Football League debut on 29 September 1923 as the Wearsiders beat Manchester City 5-2. He quickly established himself as the club's first-choice 'keeper and over the next six seasons played in 227 League and Cup games. His form was such during this period that he won a full England cap in October 1926 against Ireland at Anfield. The game ended all-square at 3-3 but McInroy was never selected again.

In October 1929 he was transferred to Newcastle United for £2,750. A well-known dressing-room comedian and exuding confidence, he was a central figure in the Magpies' journey to Wembley in 1932 when they beat Arsenal 2-1 in the FA Cup Final.

At one time during his spell on Tyneside, McInroy sustained a poisoned finger, a serious complaint which necessitated talk of amputation. Thankfully surgery was averted, though he was out of action for a long period, a critical loss for the Magpies who were relegated from the First Division. After being the club's regular 'keeper for five seasons, during which time he had made 160 appearances, he fell into dispute with the club's directors over a benefit payment and was given a free transfer, returning to Sunderland where he always felt at home.

Back at Roker Park, he failed to oust both Middleton and Thorpe and in the summer of 1935 left to join Leeds United. Though he was now at the veteran stage, McInroy turned in some highly-agile performances for the Elland Road club during his 67 appearances. After a spell with Gateshead, he kept goal for Stockton before seeing out his career with a number of junior clubs in the north-east.

On retiring soon after the Second World War, he became a publican in Newcastle, Gateshead and eventually Houghton-le-Spring.

NIGEL MARTYN

Born	11 August 1966. St Austell.
Career	St Blazey; Bristol Rovers (August 1987) Crystal Palace (November 1989) Leeds United (July 1996)
Internationals	1992 v CIS (Drew 2-2) v Hungary (Won 1-0) 1993 v Germany (Lost 1-2) 1997 v South Africa (Won 2-1) 1998 v Cameroon (Won 2-0) v Chile (Lost 0-2) v Belgium (Drew 0-0) 1999 v Czech Republic (Won 2-0) v France (Lost 0-2)

St Austell-born goalkeeper Nigel Martyn began his Football League career with Bristol Rovers whom he joined from St Blazey in the Duchy League in the summer of 1987. During his first season with the Pirates, Martyn kept 12 clean sheets in a 13-match spell and after proving himself to be one of the best 'keepers in the Third Division, won the first of eleven caps for the England Under-21 side. He had appeared in 123 League and Cup games for Bristol Rovers when in November 1989, First Division Crystal Palace paid £1 million for his services.

In his second season at Selhurst Park, the Eagles finished third in Division One, their highest-ever finish in the Football League. This was due in no small part to Nigel Martyn who in conceding just 41 goals, kept 16 clean sheets in 38 games. Not surprisingly his form led to him winning full international honours when he came on as a substitute goalkeeper for Chris Woods in the 2-2 draw against the CIS in Moscow on 29 April 1992. Two weeks later he made his first full appearance in a 1-0 win over Hungary in Budapest.

One of the most consistent goalkeepers in England, he continued to impress for Palace and in 1994-95 following a troubled summer in which he underwent an hernia operation, he was in outstanding form. After Liverpool had beaten Palace 6-1, he had a brilliant run, conceding just 29 goals with 13 clean sheets to his name before a broken index finger brought an end to 150 consecutive first team appearances.

Despite going on the transfer list at Selhurst Park, Martyn continued to produce outstanding displays for Palace where he was the longest-serving player at the club. Having helped Palace reach the play-off final he was beaten in the last minute of extra-time when Leicester City's Steve Claridge's miss-Hit volley flew past him to give the Foxes victory and the third promotion place. Martyn had appeared in 349 first team games for the Eagles when in July 1996 he joined Leeds United for £2.25 million.

In his first season at Elland Road he kept more clean sheets than any other Premier League goalkeeper and was voted United's Player of the Year.

In the wake of David Seaman's injury, he began to establish himself as England's clear second-choice goalkeeper and was one of three goalkeepers selected for England's twenty-two in the 1998 World Cup Finals in France.

Voted into the PFA award-winning Premier League side, Nigel Martyn remains a vital part of the Yorkshire club's future success.

HARRY MASKREY

Born	8 October 1880. Unstone nr Dronfield, Derbyshire
Died	21 April 1927.
Career	Ripley Athletic; Derby County (December 1902)
	Bradford City (October 1909) Ripley Town cs 1911
	Burton All Saints; Derby County (September to
	December 1920) Burton All Saints cs 1921.
Internationals	1908 v Ireland (Won 3-1)

After beginning his career with Ripley Athletic, Harry Maskrey joined Derby County where he became the third top-class goalkeeper behind John Robinson and Jack Fryer to play for the Rams.

Soon after he succeeded Jack Fryer in the County side, the former miner was described as having 'all the collier's contempt for hard knocks'. Though Maskrey was not quite as tall as the man he replaced, he was still quite a size. He stood 6ft 1ins and weighed 13 stone 2lbs and measured 77 inches from finger tip to finger tip of his outstretched arms, a physique which helped him into the Grenadier Guards during the First World War.

Agile, despite his weight and quick to sense danger, Maskrey spent just a short time in Derby's reserve side before establishing himself as the regular first team 'keeper midway through the 1903-04 season.

A very assured 'keeper, he represented the Football League against the Irish League before being capped by England against Ireland in Belfast in February 1908, a match England won 3-1.

In October 1909, Maskrey left the Baseball Ground and joined Bradford City but after two seasons at Valley Parade he returned to non-League football with Ripley Town. He returned to Derby County in an emergency in December 1920 and played in five more games for the Rams to take his total of League and Cup appearances to 222 before leaving to play for Burton All Saints. On retirement he became licensee of the New Inn in Russell Street Derby where he sadly collapsed and died aged just 46.

REG MATTHEWS

Born	20 December 1932. Coventry.
Career	Coventry City (May 1950) Chelsea (November 1956) Derby County (October 1961) Rugby Town player-manager (August 1968)
Internationals	1956 v Scotland (Drew 1-1) v Brazil (Won 4-2) v Sweden (Drew 0-0) v West Germany (Won 3-1) v N.Ireland (Drew 1-1)

Reg Matthews began his career with Coventry City, joining the High-field Road club from the groundstaff team, Modern Machine Tools on his 17th birthday in May 1950. He made his league debut against Southend United two years later but it was the 1954-55 season when he really made his name. For the first ten games of this campaign, City's goal was guarded by Peter Taylor, later to find fame as Brian Clough's right-hand managerial partner. But in the game against Leyton Orient, Taylor broke a finger and for the next game, Reg Matthews took over and was soon receiving rave reports.

As Matthews received early recognition, the crowd soon warmed to him and he became the undisputed star of an ailing Coventry side. He progressed through the England ranks at Under-23 and 'B' team level but with England having an embarrassing supply of international-class goalkeepers such as Bert Williams and Gil Merrick, many thought it would be impossible for a Third Division player to break into the England team.

However, with some stirring performances for Coventry keeping him in the headlines, he eventually made his international debut against Scotland at Hampden Park in April 1956 and gave a creditable performance in a 1-1 draw.

Matthews continued to blossom the following season and added many thousands to Third Division attendances throughout the country as fans flocked to see the lower division player who had represented his country. City directors constantly denied that he would move on but the club had struggled to maintain an average side since being relegated in the early 1950s and any player of the slightest potential was soon on the move.

Matthews made another three full international appearances before it became quite evident that the Highfield Road club were once again to cash in on their talent, despite the repeated denials. Practically overnight, Reg Matthews left the club for Chelsea for a then record fee for a goalkeeper of £22,500 in November 1956.

His move to Stamford Bridge was probably the biggest mistake Matthews ever made. Unable to settle in London he continued to live in Coventry and as a result he couldn't train with his team-mates on a regular basis. Not surprisingly he produced his best form only intermittently during his time with the Blues. His best display came in Chelsea's visit to the Midlands, with a superlative series of saves in a 2-1 win over Wolves in January 1959. However, by the closing weeks of the 1959-60 season, he was facing fierce competition from Peter Bonetti and in October 1961 after playing in 148 games he moved to Derby County for a fee of £6,300.

His acrobatic saves and courage in hurling himself at forwards' feet were loved by the County supporters and he set a club record, later beaten by Colin Boulton for goalkeeping appearances. Matthews totally dominated his own penalty area and quite often fellow defenders had to be as wary as opposing forwards ! For one season, Matthews, who played in 246 games for the Rams, kept the club in Division Two virtually single-handed.

He later worked for Massey Ferguson before having to retire through ill-health.

WILLIAM MAYNARD

Born	18 March 1853. Camberwell,London.
Died	2 September 1921.
Career	1st Surrey Rifles; Wanderers 1880-81. Also represented Surrey in 1877.
Internationals	1872 v Scotland (Drew 0-0)

William Maynard kept goal in England's very first international against Scotland at the West of Scotland Cricket Club at Partick on 30 November 1872, probably being pressed into service because Alex Morten, the original choice was unable to play. Though there was little in the way of goalmouth excitement, the crowd of 3,500 curious Scottish spectators were able to appreciate the individual skills of a number of players. That there were no goals was due to the fine displays of Maynard and his Scottish counterpart Gardner of Queen's Park.

Maynard though was primarily a forward for the 1st Surrey Rifles and his performances on the wing led to him representing Surrey in 1877. Fast and hard-working, though he sometimes delayed his centres, Maynard's second cap for England came four years after his first but this time he was on the losing side as England went down 3-0 to Scotland.

He later played for the Wanderers before hanging up his boots. He was District Registrar of Durham from 1903 to his death in September 1921. His son Alfred Frederick Maynard, who lost his life in the First World War, was an England Rugby Union internationalist.

GIL MERRICK

Born	26 January 1922. Sparkhill, Birmingham.
Career	Fenton Rovers; Shirley Juniors; Olten Sports; Solihull Town (August 1939) Birmingham City (August 1939) Birmingham City manager (June 1960 - April 1964) Bromsgrove Rovers part-time manager early 1967; Atherstone Town manager in the early 1970s.

Internationals   1951 v N.Ireland (Won 2-0) v Austria (Drew 2-2)
1952 v Scotland (Won 2-1)v Italy (Drew 1-1)
v Austria (Won 3-2) v Switzerland (Won 3-0)
v N.Ireland (Drew 2-2) v Wales (Won 5-2)
v Belgium (Won 5-0) 1953 v Scotland (Drew 2-2)
v Argentina (Drew 0-0) v Chile (Won 2-1)
v Uruguay (Lost 1-2) v Wales (Won 4-1) v Rest of
Europe (Drew 4-4) v N.Ireland (Won 3-1) v Hungary
(Lost 3-6) 1954 v Scotland (Won 4-2) v Yugoslavia
(Lost 0-1) v Hungary (Lost 1-7) v Belgium (Drew
4-4) v Switzerland (Won 2-0) v Uruguay (Lost 2-4)

Gil Merrick always modelled himself on his childhood favourite, Harry Hibbs. After playing his early football with Shirley Juniors and Solihull Town, he joined Birmingham City as a professional in the summer of 1939. Though the Second World War prevented him from making his league debut he did appear in 172 games for the Blues during the hostilities and helped the club win the League South Championship in 1945-46. He also 'guested' for a number of clubs including Nottingham Forest and West Bromwich Albion.

He eventually made his Football League debut in a 2-1 win at Tottenham Hotspur on the opening day of the 1946-47 season and missed just one game as the club finished third in Division Two. The following season he helped the club win the Second Division Championship and in 1951 won the first of 23 full caps for

England when he played in a 2-0 win over Northern Ireland at Villa Park.

At international level, Merrick was on the losing side on only five occasions, two of which were heavy defeats against Hungary.

He was Birmingham City's first-choice 'keeper for thirteen seasons and was ever-present in 1949-50 and 1950-51 when he appeared in 126 consecutive league games. He helped the Blues win the Second Division Championship again in 1954-55 and played in the 1956 FA Cup Final when they lost 3-1 to Manchester City. Merrick, who played his last game against Leeds United in October 1959, holds the St Andrew's club record for the number of first team appearances in a City shirt, a total of 551.

After retiring at the end of the 1959-60 season, he was appointed as the Blues' team manager. Almost immediately he saw City lose to Barcelona in the second leg of the Inter Cities Fairs Cup Final in Spain and remained in that country to study Spanish football methods and organisations.

On his return to St Andrew's, the club's performances improved a little but they still ended the 1960-61 season in 19th place in the First Division. After losing to AS Roma in the Fairs Cup Final carried over from the previous season, the Blues finished 17th in the top flight. In fact, they were constantly fighting against relegation during Merrick's time in office but they did beat Aston Villa over two legs to win the 1963 League Cup Final. He was sacked a year later after another season of struggle and became manager of Bromsgrove Rovers before taking charge at Atherstone Town.

JOHN MEW

Born	30 March 1889. Sunderland.
Died	16 January 1963.
Career	Blaydon United; Marley Hill Colliery; Manchester United (October 1912) Barrow (September 1926) Subsequently coached in Belgium and South America.
Internationals	1920 v Ireland (Won 2-0)

After beginning his career as a nine-year-old goalkeeper in Sunderland schoolboy football, John Mew joined Blaydon United in the Northern Alliance. Over the next two seasons, Mew, who was a virtual ever-present between the posts for Blaydon, conceded just 15 goals, prompting Sunderland to offer him professional terms. Mew turned these down and went to play for Marley Hill Colliery.

After a series of impressive displays he was invited to Old Trafford for a four-week trial after which United signed him. Mew made his league debut for the Red Devils in a 3-2 home defeat at the hands of Middlesbrough in March 1913. He played in only a handful of games before the First World War broke out due to the fine form of Harry Edmonds who had succeeded the club's regular 'keeper at the time, Harry Moger. It was during the war that Mew finally won a regular first team place, appearing in 126 wartime games for the Reds.

Mew, who had exceptionally strong wrists and excellent handling ability, toured South Africa with the 1920 FA touring party, playing once against their national team. An ever-present in 1919-20, Mew represented the Football League before winning his first full cap for England in a 2-0 win over Ireland at Sunderland in 1920. Mew was one of several goalkeepers tried by England as a possible replacement for the great Sam Hardy but despite keeping a clean sheet, he was never chosen again.

Though he was said to be on the small side for a goalkeeper, nobody at Old Trafford ever had any complaints about his ability. He left the Reds in September 1926 after making 199 League and Cup appearances to play for Barrow. A year later he left Holker Street and had coaching spells in Belgium and South America before returning to Manchester.

After ending his involvement with the game, he worked in a Manchester factory but in the mid-1920s he was in a business partnership with Cecil Parkin, the Lancashire and England cricketer.

FRED MITCHELL

Born	18 November 1897. Manchester.
Died	30 May 1975.
Career	Blackpool (1914-15) Northern Nomads; Manchester University; Preston North End (October 1920) Manchester City (May 1922) Leicester City (October 1926)
Internationals	1924 v Ireland (Won 3-1)

The son of a famous billiards player, Fred Mitchell began his Football League career with Blackpool, making his debut in March 1915 in a goalless draw at home to Lincoln City. He kept three clean sheets in five appearances for the Seasiders before the outbreak of the First World War interrupted his career.

After the hostilities had ended, Mitchell left Bloomfield Road and joined Preston North End. Still an amateur, his move to Deepdale was one of the few times when he was not the centre of attraction, for few players were as conspicuous. A wartime graduate of Manchester University, Mitchell warranted more attention than most since high academic qualifications were rare amongst footballers at that time.

Mitchell's methods were to say the least, unorthodox, for he used his feet as much as his hands. Finally, there was the feature that preserved him not just in North End folk lore but also in that of every club he played for - he sported spectacles on the field of play. Wearing spectacles was an uncommon enough sight among outfield players, but only one other goalkeeper playing in the early 1920s wore them. Mitchell was a teacher at Arnold School, Blackpool and his duties resulted in him missing a number of games. Though his appearances were both sporadic and erratic, he was in goal when North End played Huddersfield Town in the 1922 FA Cup Final.

The game at Stamford Bridge was one of the worst-ever finals and was winding its dismal way into oblivion when Billy Smith, Huddersfield's left-winger was brought down in the area by Hamilton. The referee pointed to the spot and remained that way despite a series of protests and tantrums from the Preston players. Even when the indignant players were finally cleared from the area, the acrimony was not abated. As Smith ran up to take the penalty, Fred Mitchell started to jump up and down gesticulating wildly in an astonishing display of gamesmanship. However, Smith was completely unruffled and made no mistake with the kick.

It was Mitchell's last game for Preston for in the summer he joined Manchester City. An amateur international, he had represented England at the 1920 Olympic Games in the high jump event and went on to serve City for over three seasons, appearing in 112 League and Cup games. Whilst with City, Mitchell won his one and only full international cap for England when he played in the 3-1 win over Ireland at Anfield in October 1924.

In October 1926, Mitchell left Maine Road to take up an appointment just outside Leicester with Stead and Simpson the footwear chain. He ended a distinguished football career by playing for a season in Leicester City's reserve team.

WILLIAM MOON

Born	27 June 1868. Maida Vale, London.
Died	9 January 1943.
Career	Westminster School (XI 1884-85) Old Westminsters; Corinthians (1886-1901) Also represented the London FA.
Internationals	1888 v Wales (Won 5-1) v Scotland (Won 5-0)
	1889 v Scotland (Lost 2-3) v Wales (Won 4-1)
	1890 v Wales (Won 3-1) v Scotland (Drew 1-1)
	1891 v Scotland (Won 2-1)

William Moon

William Moon began his career with Old Westminsters where his outstanding displays in goal led to him representing the London FA in 1887. In February 1888 he made the first of seven international appearances for England when he played in the 5-1 win over Wales at Crewe. The following month he kept goal on the first of four occasions against the Auld Enemy at Hampden Park, keeping a clean sheet in a 5-0 win. Moon was a goalkeeper without a superior in his hey-day, resourceful, confident, courageous and quick with both hands and feet. On his next appearance against Scotland in April 1889, Moon was in splendid form. The Scottish team showed nine changes from the last meeting between the two countries and dominated proceedings straight from the kick-off. Only the agility and bravery of William Moon kept the score to 3-2 in Scotland's favour. There is no doubt that Moon's best game for England came in his penultimate appearance against Scotland at Hampden Park when the teams drew 1-1 in April 1890. The Scots attacked the England goal incessantly for the whole of the second-half but Moon was equal to everything they could throw at him and received a standing ovation on the final whistle.

Moon, who also played for the Corinthians from 1886 to 1901 was a useful wicket-keeper/batsman and in 1891 represented Middlesex on two occasions. Brother of the Middlesex and England cricketer Leonard Moon, he too would have reached the highest level if he had been able to devote more time to the summer sport.

A solicitor by profession, he was a partner in a firm practising in Bloomsbury.

ALEXANDER MORTEN

Born	15 November 1831. Hayes
Died	24 February 1900.
Career	Crystal Palace (the original club) circa 1865-1874
	Wanderers circa 1865-1872; He also represented
	Middlesex and London in county matches and served
	on the FA Committee 1874.
Internationals	1873 v Scotland (Won 4-2)

Alexander Morten, who played for both Crystal Palace and the Wanderers, also represented both Middlesex and London in county matches. In March 1873 he became England's oldest debutant, being 41 years of age when he played in the match against Scotland at the Kennington Oval. The home side won 4-2 with Morten's Crystal Palace teammate Charles Chenery scoring one of the goals.

Morten was, in the year of his England appearance, reputedly a goalkeeper without a rival, yet twelve months later, he was said to be 'now almost retired from active service on the field but as an umpire is still held in the highest esteem.'

Also in 1874, Morten served on the FA Committee. On hanging up his boots, the Middlesex-born goalkeeper became a Stock Exchange broker in the City. He died at Earl's Court in February 1900.

FRANK MOSS

Born	5 November 1909. Leyland.
Died	7 February 1970.
Career	Lostock Hall; Leyland Motors; Preston North End (February 1928) Oldham Athletic (May 1929) Arsenal (November 1931) Heart of Midlothian manager (March 1937-1940)
Internationals	1934 v Scotland (Won 3-0) v Hungary (Lost 1-2) v Czechoslovakia (Lost 1-2) v Italy (Won 3-2)

With the exception of Birmingham's Harry Hibbs, Frank Moss was considered to be the most complete and confident goalkeeper of the 1930s. He was a brave, agile 'keeper with an uncanny sense of anticipation and kicked well with both feet.

Moss began his goalkeeping career at junior level with local teams, Lostock Hall and Leyland Motors before joining Preston North End in February 1928. He made 24 league appearances for the Deepdale club before being transferred to Oldham Athletic in May 1929.

Used mainly as an understudy to the Latics' England 'keeper Jack Hacking, Moss played in 29 league games for Oldham before leaving Boundary Park in November 1931 and joining Arsenal for a fee of £3,000.

Gunners' manager Herbert Chapman gave Moss his Arsenal debut in place of the injured Charlie Preedy against Chelsea later that month and he kept his place for the remainder of the season, helping the club to the FA Cup Final where they lost 2-1 to Newcastle United. Moss made goalkeeping look easy and his performances in his first season at Highbury earned him Football League honours.

Over the next three seasons in which Arsenal won a hat-trick of League Championships, Frank Moss missed only fifteen of the club's 126 league games. During this spell he won four full caps for England, the first against Scotland in April 1934 in a 3-0 win.

In March 1935 Moss suffered a dislocated shoulder in the match against Everton at Goodison Park and was forced to play the remainder of the game at outside-left. Moss always thought he was good enough to be an outfield player and proved this when scoring Arsenal's opening goal in a 2-0 win. Though he played in five of the following season's matches, he was still troubled by the injury and at the age of 27 was forced to retire from the game.

There is no doubt that if Moss, who had appeared in 161 League and Cup games for Arsenal, had been able to continue his career, he would have been mentioned with the likes of Banks, Clemence and Shilton.

In March 1937, Moss was appointed manager of Heart of Midlothian before leaving the post in 1940 when he was called up for war service. At the time of his death in February 1970, Moss, who had worked as a driller at Leyland Motors, was employed as a licensee at Chorley.

BEN OLNEY

Born	30 March 1899. Holborn, London.
Died	9 September 1943.
Career	Fairley's Athletic (Birmingham's works team)
	Aston Park Rangers (in this spell he signed
	amateur forms for Brierley Hill Alliance)
	Stourbridge; Derby County (April 1921) Aston
	Villa (December 1927) Bilston United (July 1930)
	Walsall (August 1931) Shrewsbury Town (August
	1932)
Internationals	1928 v France (Won 5-1) v Belgium (Won 3-1)

Nephew of Jim Olney the former Birmingham and Swansea player, he was born at Holborn, London but raised in Birmingham. He played his early football for Fairley's Athletic before and after the First World War during which he played Army football. Olney also had spells with Aston Park Rangers and Brierley Hill Alliance before joining Stourbridge in 1919. Following an impressive display for the Birmingham FA in a junior international against Scotland, he was signed by Derby County who paid £800 for his services in April 1921.

He made his league debut for the Rams in a 1-1 draw against Manchester United the following month. He established himself as the club's first-choice 'keeper at the start of the following season and between February 1922 and September 1927, Olney appeared in all but ten of Derby County's 247 League and Cup matches. One of his most outstanding performances for the Rams came in the 1923 FA Cup semi-final against West Ham United, whilst in 1925-26 he was instrumental in the Baseball Ground club winning promotion to the First Division. However, the following season he lost his place to Harry Wilkes and was languishing in the reserves when Aston Villa secured his services in December 1927.

Ironically, County had just completed their first-ever league 'double' over Aston Villa - winning 5-0 at home and 1-0 away and it was this that prompted Villa to look for a new 'keeper.

Four months after making his Villa debut, Olney won full international honours, playing in the matches against France and Belgium, which England won 5-1 and 3-1 respectively. Olney's performances for Villa kept Tommy Jackson out of the side but in the summer of 1930 after making 97 appearances for the Villans, he moved to non-League Bilston United where a year later he became manager.

In August 1931, he was secured by Walsall in an emergency, staying at Fellows Park for a season before moving to Shrewsbury Town where he ended his league career.

P

PHIL PARKES

Born	8 August 1950. Sedgeley, Staffordshire.
Career	Walsall (January 1968) Queen's Park Rangers (June 1970) West Ham United (February 1979)
Internationals	1974 v Portugal (Drew 0-0)

Phil Parkes began his Football League career with Walsall and made his debut for the Saddlers against Mansfield Town in April 1969. After just 52 games for the Fellows Park club, he moved to Queen's Park Rangers in the summer of 1970 for a fee of £15,000.

A very formidable figure as a goalkeeper, standing 6ft 3ins and weighing over 15 stone, he stayed at Loftus Road for eight seasons. His goalkeeping helped the club win promotion to the First Division in 1972-73 and then took them to the runners-up spot in the top flight in 1975-76 when they were pipped at the post by Liverpool. In April 1974, Parkes won his one and only full international cap for England when he kept a clean sheet in a goalless draw against Portugal in Lisbon. He also won six England Under-23 caps and played in one game for the England Under-21 side as an over-aged player before he moved to West Ham United for £525,000 in February 1979. At the time, it was the highest fee ever paid for a goalkeeper.

Parkes made his Hammers' debut in a 3-0 home win over Oldham Athletic, the first of 436 first team appearances in the West Ham goal.

In May 1980 he won an FA Cup winners' medal as the Hammers beat Arsenal 1-0 and was back at Wembley in March 1981 for the League Cup Final against Liverpool which the Upton Park club lost after a replay. That season, in addition, he kept 22 clean sheets as the club won the Second

Division Championship and returned to the top flight. Voted the Hammer of the Year in 1980-81, Parkes was ever-present in four of his twelve seasons with the club. Injury forced him to miss all but two months of the 1984-85 campaign but the following season he was back to his best, playing in all 42 matches as the Hammers challenged strongly for the First Division Championship. After playing in the 6-0 League Cup semi-final defeat at Oldham Athletic, Parkes made way for the Czech international 'keeper Ludek Miklosko.

Parkes, who had made 344 league appearances for West Ham, exactly the same as he had for Queen's Park Rangers, ended his playing career with three league games for Ipswich Town. One of a select band of players to have appeared in over 700 league games, he returned to Queen's Park Rangers in September 1991 as goalkeeping coach.

HAROLD PEARSON

Born	7 May 1908. Tamworth.
Died	2 November 1994.

Career	Glascote United Methodists; Belgrave WMC; Tamworth Castle; Bromsgrove Rovers; West Bromwich Albion
	(May 1925) Millwall (August 1937)
Internationals	1932 v Scotland (Won 3-0)

Harold Pearson began his league career with West Bromwich Albion, joining the Hawthorns club from Tamworth Castle FC in April 1925. When he moved in at Albion, his father Hubert, also a goalkeeper was still a player with the Baggies, having first starred between the posts in 1906.

In fact, Hubert played in the 1912 FA Cup Final and gained Second Division Championship medals with Albion in 1910-11 and 1919-20 before handing the 'keeper's jersey to his son. Hubert Pearson is unique amongst Albion goalkeepers in that he is the only player in that position to score a goal for the club in a league game - he scored two penalties in the 1911-12 season!

CARRERAS CIGARETTES

H. PEARSON
W. B. ALBION (1ST DIVISION)

Harold Pearson made his league debut for West Bromwich Albion against South Shields at the Hawthorns on 17 December 1927, a game which Albion won 3-0. In this same season, he won a junior international cap playing for England against Scotland.

He established himself in Albion's first team during the latter part of the 1929-30 season, taking over from another England international George Ashmore and thereafter was the club's first choice 'keeper until handing over the duties to Jimmy Adams and Billy Light early in 1936.

In 1930-31, Pearson won an FA Cup winners' medal when Albion beat Birmingham 2-1 in the final on their way to that unique double of winning promotion from Division Two and Cup success in the same season. He was ever-present that season and missed only one league game in the next two campaigns. After his Wembley success in 1931, he gained his only international cap the following year and in 1935 appeared in the FA Cup Final again, but on this occasion he was a loser as Sheffield Wednesday beat Albion 4-2.

After more than 300 games for the Albion, an illness forced him from the side. Unable to regain his place, he was transferred to Millwall for £300 in August 1937. In his first season with the Lions he helped them win the Third Division (South) Championship, appearing in 16 games.

Just as Millwall were promoted to Division Two, his old club West Bromwich Albion were relegated from the First Division. The two clubs met early in the 1938-39 season but it wasn't a reunion to remember as Albion won 5-1 at the Den !

During the early part of the Second World War, Pearson 'guested' in one game for West Ham United and then in April 1941, retired. He was a man who made goalkeeping look easy, being equally adept with both high and low crosses. He had a tremendous reach and could kick a ball vast distances.

After the hostilities had ended, he returned to the Hawthorns as coach from 1948 to 1952 and for the next twenty-five years or so worked in a factory next to his home in West Bromwich, attending the Hawthorns to watch Albion as often as he could. It was unfortunate that a relative of his, Harry Hibbs of Birmingham, was around otherwise he most surely would have gained more international call-ups than the solitary one he received sixty-eight years ago.

DICK PYM

| Born | 2 February 1893. Topsham, Devon. |
| Died | 16 September 1988. |

| Career | Exeter City (February 1911) Bolton Wanderers |

(June 1921) Yeovil and Petters United (May 1931)
Exeter City assistant-trainer (August 1937) also
scouted for Bolton Wanderers.

Internationals   1925 v Wales (Won 2-1) v Scotland (Lost 0-2)
                      1926 v Wales (Lost 1-3)

Dick Pym, the 'Topsham Fisherman' was born in that Devon village
in February 1893 and after leaving school earned his living from the
sea. He began his football career by playing as an amateur centre-forward for Topsham before becoming a goalkeeper. His impressive displays
for the village side led to Southern League Exeter City offering him the
opportunity to play at a higher level. Pym joined the Grecians in 1911
and went on to make 186 consecutive appearances for the St James Park
club before breaking a collarbone in an FA Cup tie against Watford.

In 1916 he joined the Devonshire Regiment and became a sergeant PTI.
Two years later he was transferred to the 8th East Surrey Regiment and was
later wounded in action.

When the hostilities ended, Pym returned to Exeter where his performances led to a number of top clubs attempting to secure his services. It was
Bolton Wanderers who managed to persuade Pym to join them in July 1921
after weeks of negotiations. Although the precise fee was never revealed, it
was believed to be around £5,000, which was a record for both clubs at the
time and a record for any goalkeeper.

He made his Football League debut for the Wanderers in a 2-2 home
draw with Preston North End and quickly settled into the team that won the
FA Cup for the first time in the famous White Horse Final of 1923. Pym's
qualities were soon recognised and he appeared for the Football League
against the Irish League in Belfast yet incredibly, despite his seafaring back-
ground, he was seasick on the crossing from Liverpool !

In February 1925, Pym won the first of three England caps when he played
against Wales at Swansea's Vetch Field ground. The following year he collected another FA Cup winners' medal as Bolton beat Manchester City 1-0 and
despite injury, made it a hat-trick of Wembley wins in 1929 as Wanderers
defeated Portsmouth 2-0, to make it three clean sheets in his FA Cup Final
appearances. Pym played the last of his 336 League and Cup games for the
Trotters at Anfield in September 1930, a match the Wanderers lost 7-2 !

On retiring from the game, Pym returned to the fishing industry in
Topsham where he remained until his death in September 1988, the last
survivor of the 1923 FA Cup winning side.

R

GEORGE RAIKES

Born	14 March 1873. Carleton-Forhoe, Norfolk.
Died	18 December 1966.
Career	Shrewsbury School (XI 1890-1892) Oxford University (Blue 1893-94-95-96) Corinthians 1893-1896; Wymondham FC. Also appeared in Norfolk's county team.
Internationals	1895 v Wales (Drew 1-1) 1896 v Ireland (Won 2-0) v Wales (Won 9-1) v Scotland (Lost 1-2)

After prominence at Shrewsbury School where he was a member of the first XI from 1890 to 1892, George Raikes played for Oxford University, winning his Blue. He also turned out for Corinthians and Wymondham FC in his home county of Norfolk but it was whilst at Oxford University that he won his four caps for England.

He made his international debut in March 1895 in a 1-1 draw against Wales at the Queen's club in London. After keeping a clean sheet in a 2-0 win over Ireland, he was a member of the side that beat Wales 9-1 in March 1896 before ending his international career with an outstanding display against Scotland at Hampden Park the following month.

After leaving university in the summer of 1896, Raikes, who was just 23 years old, decided to retire from first-class football ! Also a noted cricketer, his impressive performances for Norfolk led to him playing first-class cricket for Hampshire and in nine matches he scored 409 runs and captured 25 wickets. Raikes was ordained in 1897 and curate of Portsea until 1903. He was chaplain to the Duke of Portland from 1905 to 1920 and then Rector of Bergh Apton, Norfolk until his retirement in 1936.

JOHN RAWLINSON

Born	21 December 1860. New Alresford, Hampshire.
Died	14 January 1926.
Career	Eton College, Cambridge University (Blue 1882-83) Old Etonians; Corinthians; Served on the FA Committee 1885-86.
Internationals	1882 v Ireland (Won 13-0)

Educated at Eton College, John Rawlinson went up to Cambridge University, where he won a Blue in 1882 and 1883. An important member of the Old Etonians side, he appeared in three successive FA Cup Finals for them from 1881 to 1883. When Old Etonians reached the Kennington Oval final in 1881, Rawlinson was on the losing side as Old Carthusians beat them 3-0. The following year he won an FA Cup winners' medal as Old Etonians beat Blackburn Rovers 1-0 but was again on the losing side twelve months later as Blackburn Olympic defeated the Old Etonains 2-1 after extra-time.

Rawlinson was a sound, cool custodian, though at times, the coolness was reported to border on casualness !

In February 1882 he won his only full cap for England when he played in the match against Ireland at Belfast. He had very little to do in a 1-0 win, only touching the ball on a couple of occasions !

That same year he served on the original committee of the Corinthians and in 1885-86 was a member of the FA Committee.

A barrister by profession, being called to the Bar in 1884 and a Q.C from 1897, Rawlinson was Recorder of Cambridge and M.P for Cambridge University from 1906 until his death some twenty years later.

JOE READER

Born	27 February 1866. West Bromwich.
Died	8 March 1954.
Career	Carters Green FC cs 1884; West Bromwich Albion (January 1885) Later served Albion as trainer and coach and then as steward.
Internationals	1894 v Ireland (Drew 2-2)

A goalkeeper to rank with the finest the game has produced, Joe Reader joined West Bromwich Albion from Carters Green FC in January 1885. He made his debut for the Baggies in a 1-0 defeat at Aston Villa in October 1889, taking over from the great Bob Roberts.

Superb in handling and with marvellous reflexes, Reader used his feet as much as anything else to divert goalbound shots or headers. He played for Albion in the 1892 FA Cup Final when they beat Aston Villa 3-0 where his display as the Villans pressed for an equaliser, was outstanding. He was also in goal in the 1895 FA Cup Final when Villa gained their revenge with a 1-0 win. That year, Reader was sent-off in the league game at Bolton, the only Albion goalkeeper to receive his marching orders.

Reader's only international cap came in March 1894 when he kept goal in the 2-2 draw against Ireland in Belfast. He also represented the Football League three times and played for a League XI once.

A dedicated clubman, he turned out in one match with his arm in a sling ! Nicknamed 'Kicker' he is the only West Bromwich Albion player to have served the club on three different home grounds - Four Acres, Stoney Lane and the Hawthorns.

He was Albion's goalkeeper for 16 years and was forced to give up the game through illness rather than injury in 1901. It is believed that Joe Reader was the last of the 'keepers to discard the customary long white trousers, doing so in the mid-1890s.

A keen and active member of the club during his spell as coach until shortly before the First World War, he later became a steward, a position he held until 1950 - his association with West Bromwich Albion thus spanning 65 years !

JIMMY RIMMER

Born	10 February 1948. Southport.
Career	Manchester United (May 1965) Swansea City on loan (October 1973-February 1974) Arsenal (March 1974) Aston Villa (August 1977) Swansea City (July 1983) Luton Town (October 1986)
Internationals	1976 v Italy (Won 3-2)

Jimmy Rimmer joined Manchester United straight from school as a 15-year-old in 1963 and graduated through the Reds' junior teams, winning an FA Youth Cup winners' medal in 1964. After making his first team debut for United in their 1967 tour of Australia, he was given his first taste of Football League action in April 1968 when he played in the 3-0 win against Fulham. He was the substitute goalkeeper in the 1968 European Cup Final against Benfica and spent most of his time as understudy to Alex Stepney before being loaned to Swansea in October 1973. Harry Gregg, the former United and Northern Ireland 'keeper who was manager at the Vetch Field improved Rimmer's game before returning him to Old Trafford. Though he only played in 17 games in that loan spell, he soon influenced the team's performances, so much that in February 1974, Arsenal paid Manchester United £40,000 for Rimmer's services.

The new recruit impressed by keeping a clean sheet in an unexpected victory against Liverpool at Anfield and with Bob Wilson retiring at the end of the season, the Southport-born 'keeper grabbed his opportunity. During his three seasons at Highbury, he showed great consistency, missing only three league matches. He won an England cap against Italy on the American tour of 1976. However, when Pat Jennings joined the Gunners in August 1977, Rimmer realised that his days at Highbury were over and during the same week, after making 146 League and Cup appearances for Arsenal, he was transferred to Aston Villa for £80,000.

He served the Midlands club for six seasons, helping them win both the League Championship and the European Cup, although in the final of the latter competition, he was injured after ten minutes and had to be replaced. Rimmer went on to play in 285 games for Villa before losing his place to the up and coming Nigel Spink. He left Villa Park in the summer of 1983 to rejoin Swansea City. He went on to appear in 83 league games for the Swans before becoming Youth team coach at the Vetch.

BOB ROBERTS

Born	25 April 1859. West Bromwich.
Died	28 October 1929.

Career	Salter's Works; West Bromwich Albion (September 1879) Sunderland Albion (May 1890) West Bromwich Albion (May 1891) Aston Villa (May 1892)
Internationals	1887 v Scotland (Lost 2-3) 1888 v Ireland (Won 5-1) 1890 v Ireland (Won 9-1)

West Bromwich Albion's first international player, Bob Roberts, like many of the club's pioneers was a pupil of Christ Church School in the town and an employee of the George Salter factory which was part of the club's formation. He was the goalkeeper when the club under the name of West Bromwich Strollers played their first game on 23 November 1878 against Hudson's Works side and kept a clean sheet in a goalless draw.

During the club's early days, he tried several outfield positions before settling down as a goalkeeper. He certainly had the build for it - 13 stone and 6ft 4ins and taking a size 13 boot - for in those days 'keepers had to be pretty bulky to prevent opposing forwards from bundling them and the ball over the line !

Bob Roberts was Albion's goalkeeper in three successive FA Cup Finals from 1886 to 1888, collecting a winners' medal in the last of these finals as Albion beat Preston North End 2-1 at Kennington Oval. It was his performance in the first of these finals that helped him win the first of three full caps for England when he was chosen to play against Scotland at Blackburn in March 1887.

He was also Albion's goalkeeper in their first Football League game in September 1888, keeping a clean sheet in a 2-0 win over Stoke. He went on to miss just three games in the first two seasons of the competition before being persuaded to sign for another Albion - Sunderland Albion - at the end of the 1889-90 season. However, he was unable to settle in the north-east and after just one season he returned to Stoney Lane to play for West Bromwich.

The Albion had just won the FA Cup again, beating Aston Villa 3-0 and Roberts couldn't displace his former deputy Joe Reader, who had played well in the final. He left the club once more, ending his playing career as Villa's reserve 'keeper after one season there. He then returned to the north-east where he worked as a plasterer.

JACK ROBINSON

Born	22 April 1870. Derby.
Died	28 October 1931.

Career	Derby Midland; Lincoln City; Derby County cs 1891; New Brighton Tower (August 1897) Southampton (May 1898) Plymouth Argyle (May 1903) Exeter City (October 1905) Millwall Athletic (November 1905) Green Waves FC cs 1907; Exeter City (September 1908) Stoke (May 1909)
Internationals	1897 v Ireland (Won 6-0) v Scotland (Lost 1-2) 1898 v Ireland (Won 3-2) v Wales (Won 3-0) v Scotland (Won 3-1) 1899 v Wales (Won 4-0) v Scotland (Won 2-1) 1900 v Ireland (Won 2-0) v Wales (Drew 1-1) v Scotland (Lost 1-4) 1901 v Ireland (Won 3-0)

Jack Robinson was a spectacular goalkeeper of unquestionable brilliance who was considered to have the safest pair of hands in England at the turn of the last century.

He began his distinguished career at Derby Midland and then Lincoln City before signing for Derby County in June 1891. He spent six excellent seasons at the Baseball Ground and had broken into the England team playing his first international against Ireland at Nottingham in February 1897. In August of that year, he not only rocked his club but the whole of football by joining New Brighton Tower who were outside the FA's jurisdiction at that time. Only after New Brighton joined the FA via the Cheshire FA did the transfer go through and a contemporary report gave the opinion: 'If Robinson thinks he can enhance his reputation by joining a mushroom organisation like the New Brighton club, whose purse may not always be so heavy as it is at present, he has done well to leave Derby'. It did not do Robinson any harm for he retained his England place and a year later joined Southampton.

He soon showed his bravery, when in an important deciding match against Bristol City he badly sprained his hand but refused to leave the field. At the Dell, he took his total of England caps to eleven, played in the 1902 FA Cup Final and won three Southern League Championship medals in 1898-99, 1900-01 and 1902-03. Whilst with the Saints, Robinson was again in conflict with the football authorities. He was reported to the FA for trying to poach Steve Bloomer for Southampton whilst he was still at Derby.

In May 1903 he moved to Plymouth Argyle and followed this by playing for Millwall, Exeter City, Plymouth Argyle (second spell) and Exeter City (second spell) before finally ending his career with Stoke.

He was 43 years old when he joined the Potters and when he made his debut in an 11-0 win over Merthyr Tydfil, he became one of the club's oldest debutants. He served the club well for two seasons, helping them win the Southern League Division Two play-off. In 1912 he emigrated to the United States and played with Rochester until he was 49. He kept a pub in Southampton for a while, returning to live in Turnditch near Derby just before his death.

BILLY ROSE

Born	4 March 1861. St Pancras, London.
Died	4 February 1937.
Career	Small Heath; Swifts; Preston North End (February 1885) Stoke; Wolverhampton Wanderers (1888-89) Loughborough Town (May 1894) Wolverhampton Wanderers cs 1895;
Internationals	1884 v Ireland (Won 8-1) v Scotland (Lost 0-1) v Wales (Won 4-0) 1886 v Ireland (Won 6-1) 1891 v Ireland (Won 6-1)

Billy Rose had made a name for himself in London when playing for the Swifts club, having started off his career in goal for the Midlands club, Small Heath. During the mid 1880s, he represented Wiltshire, London and Staffordshire in county matches and was by far the best 'custodian' in the land at that time.

Standing over 6 feet tall and weighing 12 stone, Billy Rose was strong, lively and enthusiastic. He was a real character both on and off the field and was always on the go - often putting the fear of God into his opponents by the way he used to race out of his goal into their path as they attacked down the centre of the field.

In the summer of 1885, he left London to join Preston North End but after just one season with the Lancashire club, he switched to Stoke before three years later moving to Wolverhampton Wanderers.

Rose, who had been capped four times by England before he joined the Molineux club - lining up against Ireland in February 1884 (when he finished up on the winning side as England won 8-1) v Scotland and Wales the following month and against Ireland again in March 1886. He became Wolves' first international goalkeeper when he added a fifth cap to his collection in March 1891 when he made it a hat-trick of appearances against the Irish. He conceded a mere four goals in his five internationals, only being on the losing side once against Scotland.

He went on to play in 155 League and Cup games for Wolves, making his last appearance in a 7-2 win over Small Heath in 1896, after which he decided to retire following an injury to his left knee.

He did however much to his own annoyance and indeed to the fans' disapproval, spend a season away from Molineux in 1894-95 when he assisted Loughborough Town, this after a disagreement with the club's committee following his proposal to form a Players' Union.

After leaving Wolves in 1896, Billy Rose became a licensee, first in Birmingham and later in Wolverhampton. He also ran a shop near St Andrew's, home of Birmingham City before dying at his home in Bordesley Green in February 1937, aged 75.

BILL ROWLEY

Born	1865. Hanley.
Died	1939
Career	Hanley Orion; Burslem Port Vale; Stoke cs 1887-1896 when he became club secretary; Leicester Fosse secretary (August 1898)
Internationals	1889 v Ireland (Won 6-1) 1892 v Ireland (Won 2-0)

Bill Rowley started his football career as a centre-forward with Hanley Orion before joining Stoke in 1883, five years before the Football

League commenced. He stayed with Stoke until April 1884 when he left to join Burslem Port Vale.

He soon became a regular in the team and when Vale demolished Ironbridge 12-0 in the final oft he Burslem Challenge Cup, he became bored and joined the attack, even scoring one of the goals ! He was also a member of the side which shared the North Staffordshire Charity Challenge Cup in 1885.

However, he broke a rib in the 3-1 defeat at Stoke in a friendly match in May 1886 and was unable to work for four months. Nevertheless he returned to the Victoria Ground in August of that year but it was in the midst of fierce controversy.

Rowley rejoined Stoke despite signing a contract to play for Burslem Port Vale and in November of that year, the matter went to court. Vale's position was upheld and Stoke were obliged to pay £20 to a Burslem charity and released Rowley back to Vale. He stayed at Stoke for all this and made his debut in an FA Cup tie against Caernarvon Wanderers which was won 10-1.

Bill Rowley was a fine and fearless goalkeeper though he did suffer a number of injuries in his career. His performances earned him numerous representative appearances for Staffordshire and then on the national stage he played for the Football League and eventually for England in 1889 in a 6-1 win over Ireland. His second cap came in 1892 when Ireland were again the opponents but despite the game being on Irish soil, England still won 2-0.

Rowley had been Stoke's goalkeeper when the team romped away with the 1890-91 Football Alliance Championship. He became club secretary in 1895 as his first team appearances started to reduce. He was technically an amateur at this point so he could serve the club as secretary.

As club secretary he caused controversy again in 1898 when Leicester Fosse paid him a signing-on fee after he'd negotiated his own transfer and prior to his single appearance in a 3-2 win.

A month later, Leicester were fined £10 and Rowley and the Leicester secretary were both suspended by the FA for twelve months. After his Fosse move had soured, Rowley was successively a postman and a licensee in Stoke before emigrating to the United States.

S

TED SAGAR

Born	7 February 1910. Moorends, Doncaster.
Died	16 October 1986.
Career	Thorne Colliery; Everton (March 1929)
Internationals	1935 v Ireland (Won 3-1) 1936 v Scotland (Drew 1-1) v Austria (Lost 1-2) v Belgium (Lost 2-3)

One of the greatest goalkeepers of all-time, Ted Sagar's career as an Everton player spanned over twenty-four years during which time he played in 495 League and Cup games. But for a lack of foresight on the part of Hull City, Sagar would never have found his way to Goodison Park.

As a youngster he was playing with Thorne Colliery in the Doncaster Senior League when he was spotted by a Tigers' scout. He was given a trial by the Boothferry Park club but they were slow to offer him a contract, so allowing Everton to nip in and sign him from under their noses.

Sagar made his Everton debut in a 4-0 home win over Derby County on 18 January 1930 and his last league appearance in a 1-0 defeat at Plymouth Argyle on 15 November 1952.

Combining sheer athleticism with bravery and tremendous vision, Sagar's handling, particularly of crosses was exemplary. It was his misfortune to have been a contemporary of Harry Hibbs and Vic Woodley, otherwise he would have won far more than the four England caps that came his way.

When Everton won the League Championship in 1931-32, Sagar

missed just one game. He was first choice until the outbreak of the Second World War, keeping a clean sheet at Wembley in 1933 to win an FA Cup winners' medal and added a second Championship medal in 1938-39, Slim and perhaps even underweight for a goalkeeper in the days when it was legitimate for centre-forwards to bounce both 'keeper and ball into the net, Sagar survived by skill alone. He had the uncanny ability to judge the high flight of the ball and was completely without nerves. Famous for launching himself headlong at the ball, regardless of the number of players blocking his path, he made his farewell appearance against Tranmere Rovers in the Liverpool Senior Cup Final.

JOHN SANDS

Born   4 March 1859. Nottingham.
Died   29 February 1924.

Career   Nottingham Forest (1878-1883)
Internationals 1880 v Wales (Won 3-2)

After playing junior football for a number of local clubs, Nottingham-born goalkeeper John Sands joined Nottingham Forest and played his first game for them in November 1878. He assisted Forest for over five years, during which time he appeared in 13 FA Cup ties for the club, helping them reach the semi-final stage of the competition on two occasions. The first in 1878-79 saw Forest lose 2-1 to Old Etonians whilst in 1879-80 they went down 1-0 to Oxford University, both matches being played at the Kennington Oval.

As a goalkeeper, John Sands was deemed 'very good' by that most demanding of critics, C.W.Alcock who was mindful of his agility and soundness. Alcock of course was the man responsible for founding the FA Cup.

In March 1880, Sands won his only England cap when he played in the 3-2 win over Wales at Wrexham's Racecourse Ground. His Forest team-mate Edwin Luntley was at full-back, whilst the other Forest player to win international honours that season was Sam Widdowson, the inventor of the shin pad.

Sands' last appearance for Forest was on 13 January 1883 when they lost 3-2 at Sheffield Wednesday in an FA Cup third round replay.

ARTHUR SAVAGE

Born   18 October 1850. Sydney, Australia.
Died   15 August 1905.

Career   Crystal Palace (original club) he also represented Surrey.
Internationals 1876 v Scotland (Lost 0-3)

Arthur Savage played for the original Crystal Palace club where his performances led to him winning representative honours for Surrey before in March 1876 he was capped by England in the match against Scotland. The partly flooded West of Scotland Cricket Club at Partick was in a dire state for the fifth official meeting of the two countries. Despite some early English pressure, the home side gradually got on top and by half-time led 3-0. England again had chances to reduce the arrears but failed to take them and as the game headed towards the final whistle, Savage redeemed himself with an outstanding save from McGeoch the Scottish 'keeper who had joined his forwards to try his luck !

Savage was a reliable custodian. He had a remarkably hefty kick but quite often this advantage was nullified by indiscriminate placing !

It was thought that the England 'keeper was the Arthur Savage of the English and Oriental Hotel, Penang but recent research has shown that he was probably Arthur Henry Patrick Savage, born in Sydney in October 1850 and who died in Bayswater in August 1905, for match reports of the time often listed the player as A.H.P. Savage.

ERNALD SCATTERGOOD

Born	29 May 1887. Riddings, Derbyshire.
Died	2 July 1932.
Career	Riddings St James; Ripley Athletic; Derby County (August 1907) Bradford (October 1914)
Internationals	1913 v Wales (Won 4-3)

After beginning his career with Ripley Athletic, Ernald Scattergood - yet another in the long line of Derbyshire produced goalkeepers - joined Derby County where he took over from Harry Maskrey. Though on the small side, he had a safe pair of hands and punched well.

In 1911-12, Scattergood was Derby County's only ever-present as the Rams won the Second Division Championship with 54 points.

The following season was quite an eventful one for Scattergood, for he not only became the club's regular penalty-taker but also represented England at full international level against Wales at Bristol City's Ashton Gate ground. In a match England won 4-3, Scattergood made a number of outstanding saves late in the game as Wales pressed for an equaliser.

As a penalty-taker for the Rams, Scattergood scored three out of three, preferring to blast the ball home rather than rely on astute placing! He had appeared in 192 League and Cup games for the Baseball Ground club when in October 1914 he was allowed to leave and join Bradford Park Avenue.

His career with the Yorkshire club was interrupted by the First World War during which he survived being gassed. Thankfully he was fit to resume between the posts for Bradford when League football returned in 1919-20, going on to play in 288 games for them. He took Park Avenue's penalties and had scored with five successive spot-kicks prior to the game against South Shields on Easter Saturday 1922. His effort in this game was saved by Willis Walker, resulting in Scattergood being involved in a frantic and successful race to return to his own line !

His son Ken, also a custodian played League football for Stoke City and Derby County during the 1930s.

DAVID SEAMAN

Born	19 September 1963. Rotherham.
Career	Leeds United (September 1981) Peterborough United (August 1982) Birmingham City (October 1984) Queen's Park Rangers (August 1986) Arsenal (May 1990)
Internationals	1989 v Saudi Arabia (Drew 1-1) v Denmark (Drew 1-1) 1990 v Czechoslovakia (Won 4-2) 1991 v Cameroon (Won 2-0) v Republic of Ireland (Drew 1-1) v Turkey (Won 1-0) v Argentina (Drew 2-2) 1992 v Czechoslovakia (Drew 2-2) v Hungary (Won 1-0) 1994 v Poland (Won 3-0) v Holland (Lost 0-2) v San Marino (Won 7-1) v Denmark (Won 1-0) v Norway (Drew 0-0) 1995 v United States (Won 2-0) v Romania (Drew 1-1) v Republic of Ireland (Lost 0-1) 1996 v Colombia (Drew 0-0) v Norway (Drew 0-0) v Switzerland (Won 3-1) v Poland (Won 2-0) v Bulgaria (Won 1-0) v Croatia (Drew 0-0) v Hungary (Won 3-0) v Switzerland (Drew 1-1) v Scotland (Won 2-0) v Holland (Won 4-1) v Spain

(Drew 0-0) v Germany (Drew 1-1) 1997 v Moldova
(Won 3-0) v Poland (Won 2-0) v Georgia (Won 2-0)
v Georgia (Won 2-0) v Poland (Won 2-0) v France
(Won 1-0) v Brazil (Lost 0-1) 1998 v Moldova
(won 4-0) v Italy (Drew 0-0) v Portugal (Won 3-0)
v Saudi Arabia (Drew 0-0) v Tunisia (Won 2-0)
v Romania (Lost 1-2) v Colombia (Won 2-0)
v Argentina (Drew 2-2) 1999 v Sweden (Drew 0-0)
v Bulgaria (Drew 0-0) v Luxembourg (Won 3-0)
v France (Lost 0-2) v Poland (Won 3-1) v Hungary
(Drew 1-1) v Sweden (Drew 0-0) v Bulgaria (Drew
1-1)

David Seaman began his career with Leeds United after he had represented Rotherham Schoolboys. He became an apprentice at Elland Road in March 1980, turning professional in September 1981. Unable to break into the Yorkshire club's first team because of the consistency of John Lukic, he was transferred to Peterborough United for £4,000 in August 1982. His brilliant form for 'The Posh' was noted by Birmingham City manager Jim Smith who paid £100,000 for his services in October 1984.

After making his debut for the Blues in a 2-0 defeat at Brighton he helped them win promotion to the First Division with a series of outstanding displays. However, in 1985-86 despite being ever-present and winning England Under-21 honours, he could not save City from relegation and in order to remain playing in the top flight, he joined Queen's Park Rangers for £225,000 in August 1986.

In four seasons at Loftus Road he was a first team fixture and in 1988-89 he won the first of his 52 caps for England when appearing against Saudi Arabia.

In May 1990 after he had appeared in 175 League and Cup games for Queen's Park Rangers, Arsenal paid out a record British fee for a goalkeeper of £1.3 million when obtaining Seaman's services.

No Gunners supporters could have realised the impact that David Seaman would have on the Arsenal side and the League Championship winning season of 1990-91 when he was ever-present, he broke two records. Seaman conceded only eighteen league goals and kept 24 clean sheets ! Again ever-present in 1991-92, he followed this in the next season by helping the club to the FA Cup and Coca Cola Cup double. In

fact, it was Seaman alone who had kept the club in the Coca Cola Cup when saving three penalties in a penalty shoot-out against Millwall at the Den.

In 1993-94 he was a key member of the side which won the European Cup Winners' Cup again Parma, this after he had battled on bravely with a painful rib injury which resulted in him having to have six pain-killing injections before the final ! In the European Cup Winners' Cup semi-final against Sampdoria, his performance in the penalty shoot-out was nothing less than miraculous and his save from Lombardo will linger long in the memory of those who saw it. After the Gunners lost to Real Zaragoza in the final where Nayim scored a wonder goal, lobbing Seaman from almost the halfway line, things got worse for the England 'keeper when he suffered a serious leg injury on Arsenal's close season tour of China.

An ever-present in 1995-96 he enhanced his reputation even more in Euro '96 with two superb penalty saves, one against Scotland in the group match and the other in a quarter-final shoot-out against Spain that were instrumental in England reaching the semi-final stage.

Unfortunately, 1996-97 was an injury ravaged season for David Seaman when he was yet again troubled by persistent rib trouble. He returned to the Arsenal side the following season and was in outstanding form, helping the Gunners to do the 'double', winning the Premier League Championship and the FA Cup when they beat Newcastle United 2-0.

In the World Cup Finals in France in the summer of 1998, Seaman appeared in all four games before a ten-man England were beaten on penalties by Argentina after he had saved one of the five taken, having earlier been booked for bringing down Diego Simeone for a dubious fifth minute penalty that was converted by Gabriel Batistuta.

A model of consistency behind Arsenal's back-four, he has kept a high percentage of clean sheets in his 421 first team appearances. Very relaxed and composed both on and off the field of play, he continues to play a big part in the tremendous team spirit which exists at Highbury.

RONNIE SEWELL

Born	19 July 1890. Middlesbrough.
Died	4 February 1945.
Career	Wingate Albion; Gainsborough Trinity (cs 1911) Burnley (February 1913) Blackburn Rovers (February 1920) Gainsborough Trinity (September 1927)
Internationals	1924 v Wales (Lost 1-2)

Ronnie Sewell began his Football League career with Wingate Albion before joining Gainsborough Trinity. His transfer to Burnley in February 1913 caused a sensation as the entire Gainsborough defence joined the Clarets following an FA Cup tie between the two clubs!

At Turf Moor, he was understudy to the Clarets' England 'keeper Jerry Dawson but won an FA Cup medal in 1914 when he deputised for him in the final, keeping a clean sheet in a 1-0 win over Liverpool. When league football resumed in 1919-20, Sewell still found his first team opportunities limited and midway through the campaign, made the short move to Blackburn Rovers. He made his debut in a 3-0 defeat at Liverpool but kept his place until the end of the season, his six clean sheets in 15 appearances helping Rovers avoid relegation to the Second Division.

Over the next two seasons, he missed just two games but in 1922-23 he lost his place to the up-and-coming Ted Davis. In fact, it was only an injury to Davis in the match against Cardiff City that restored Sewell to the Rovers' first team. Determined to hang on to his place, Sewell performed better than ever and in March 1924 made his England debut in a 2-1 defeat against Wales on his own ground of Ewood Park.

Sewell was a first team regular with Rovers for seven seasons, holding off the challenge of much younger men. A great believer in his own ability, Sewell was something of a perfectionist, unflappable under pressure and with a temperament that allowed him to ignore mistakes no matter how costly. In September 1926 in the match against Bury which Rovers won 2-0, Sewell broke his leg and though he made five appearances the following season to take his total of League and Cup outings for Rovers to 248, he was forced to retire. A one-time seafarer, Ronnie Sewell was a Lincoln licensee for a long time up to his death.

PETER SHILTON

Born   18 September 1949. Leicester.

Career   Leicester City (September 1966) Stoke City
               (November 1974) Nottingham Forest (September 1977)
               Southampton (August 1982) Derby County (July 1987)
               Plymouth Argyle (March 1992) Wimbledon (February
               1995) Bolton Wanderers (March 1995) Coventry City
               (July 1995) West Ham United (January 1996) Leyton
               Orient (November 1996)

Internationals 1970 v East Germany (Won 3-1) 1971 v Wales (Drew
               0-0) v Switzerland (Drew 1-1) 1972 v N.Ireland
               (Lost 0-1) v Yugoslavia (Drew 1-1) 1973 v Scotland
               (Won 5-0) v N.Ireland (Won 2-1) v Wales (Won 3-0)
               v Scotland (Won 1-0) v Czechoslovakia (Drew 1-1)
               v Poland (Lost 0-2) v Soviet Union (Won 2-1)
               v Italy (Lost 0-2) v Austria (Won 7-0) v Poland
               (Drew 1-1) v Italy (Lost 0-1) 1974 v Wales (Won
               2-0) v N.Ireland (Won 1-0) v Scotland (Lost 0-2)
               v Argentina (Drew 2-2) 1975 v Cyprus (Won 5-0)
               1977 v N.Ireland (Won 2-1) v Wales (Lost 0-1)
               1978 v Wales (Won 3-1) v Hungary (Won 4-1)
               v Czechoslovakia (Won 1-0) 1979 v Sweden (Drew
               0-0) v Austria (Lost 3-4) v N.Ireland (Won 5-1)
               1980 v Spain (Won 2-0) v Italy (Lost 0-1)
               v Norway (Won 4-0) v Switzerland (Won 2-1)
               1981 v Romania (Drew 0-0) v Hungary (Won 1-0)
               1982 v Holland (Won 2-0) v Scotland (Won 1-0)
               v Finland (Won 4-1) v France (Won 3-1)
               v Czechoslovakia (Won 2-0) v Kuwait (Won 1-0)
               v W.Germany (Drew 0-0) v Spain (Drew 0-0)
               v Denmark (Drew 2-2) v W.Germany (Lost 1-2)
               v Greece (Won 3-0) 1983 v Wales (Won 2-1)
               v Greece (Drew 0-0) v Hungary (Won 2-0)
               v N.Ireland (Drew 0-0) v Scotland (Won 2-0)
               v Australia (Drew 0-0) v Australia (Won 1-0)
               v v Australia (Drew 1-1) v Denmark (Lost 0-1)
               v Hungary (Won 3-0) 1984 v France (Lost 0-2)

v N.Ireland (Won 1-0) v Wales (Lost 0-1)
v Scotland (Drew 1-1) v Soviet Union (Lost 0-2)
v Brazil (Won 2-0) v Uruguay (Lost 0-2) v Chile
(Drew 0-0) v E.Germany (Won 1-0) v Finland (Won
5-0) v Turkey (Won 8-0) v N.Ireland (Won 1-0)
1985 v Romania (Drew 0-0) v Finland (Drew 1-1)
v Scotland (Lost 0-1) v Italy (Lost 1-2) v West
Germany (Won 3-0) v Romania (Drew 1-1) v Turkey
(Won 5-0) v N.Ireland (Drew 0-0) 1986 v Egypt
(Won 4-0) v Israel (Lost 1-2) v Soviet Union
(Won 1-0) v Scotland (Won 2-1) v Mexico (Won 3-0)
v Canada (Won 1-0) v Portugal (Lost 0-1)
v Morocco (Drew 0-0) v Poland (Won 3-0) v Paraguay
(Won 3-0) v Argentina (Lost 1-2) v N.Ireland (Won
3-0) v Sweden (Lost 0-1) 1987 v Spain (Won 4-2)
v Brazil (Drew 1-1) v W.Germany (Lost 1-3)
v Turkey (Won 8-0) v Yugoslavia (Won 4-1)
1988 v Holland (Drew 2-2) v Scotland (Won 1-0)
v Colombia (Drew 1-1) v Switzerland (Won 1-0)
v Republic of Ireland (Lost 0-1) v Holland (Lost
1-3) 1989 v Denmark (Won 1-0) v Sweden (Drew 0-0)
v Greece (Won 2-1) v Albania (Won 2-0) v Albania
(Won 5-0) v Chile (Drew 0-0) v Scotland (Won 2-0)
v Poland (Drew 0-0) v Denmark (Drew 1-1) 1990
v Sweden (Drew 0-0) v Poland (Won 2-0) v Italy
(Drew 0-0) v Yugoslavia (Won 2-1) v Brazil
(Won 1-0) v Czechoslovakia (Won 4-2) v Denmark
(Won 1-0) v Uruguay (Lost 1-2) v Tunisia (Drew
1-1) v Republic of Ireland (Drew 1-1) v Holland
(Drew 0-0) v Egypt (Won 1-0) v Belgium (Won 1-0)
v Cameroon (Won 3-2) v West Germany (Drew 1-1)

Undoubtedly one of the greatest goalkeepers in the modern era, Peter Shilton trained as hard as any and his dedication to fitness and keeping his abilities at a peak, ensured one of the longest careers in recent times. Indeed other than Stanley Matthews, no one can beat the length of Shilton's England career.

He holds the English appearance record with 125 caps and only a few years ago was surpassed as the most capped in his position throughout the world of football by Swedish number one Thomas Ravelli.

A schoolboy prodigy, he helped Leicester Boys to their 1965 Trophy win and picked up his first international recognition with England Schools. At Filbert Street there was immediate acknowledgement of Shilton's precocious talent and he became Leicester City's youngest-ever First Division debutant at the age of 16, when characteristically he kept a clean sheet against Everton. He continued to make great progress to the point where he put Leicester boss Matt Gillies under pressure to play him in the first team at the expense of England international Gordon Banks or let him go. In the end, Gillies sold Banks and Shilton started to accumulate appearances and records, after making his England debut against East Germany in November 1970.

In the interim, the Foxes had experienced a Cup Final, and a relegation but in 1970-71 they won the Second Division Championship with Shilton creating the club's best-ever defensive record when he kept a record 23 clean sheets. He was rarely out of the public eye - his adoption of an all-white playing kit and his long-distance scoring success at Southampton at various times assured that !

He also became less than enchanted with Leicester's trophy-winning prospects and in November 1974 after appearing in 339 games for the Filbet Street club, he joined Stoke City for £325,000, then a world record fee for a goalkeeper.

The move ironically threatened to rebound on him as the Potters themselves struggled and he found himself only sharing the yellow jersey of England with Ray Clemence. But when Stoke dropped into Division Two, Shilton was the subject of a typically shrewd piece of business by Brian Clough who paid £240,000 for his services.

In terms of honours, he enjoyed his best years with Nottingham Forest, winning back his England place from Ray Clemence and being selected as the PFA 'Player of the Year' in 1978, gaining a League Championship medal, a League Cup and two European Cup winner' medals. He left Forest in August 1982 after playing in 272 League and Cup games to join Southampton for £300,000.

In 1983-84 he was ever-present, keeping 18 clean sheets as the Saints finished that campaign as First Division runners-up to Liverpool. Whilst at the Dell he became the most-capped England 'keeper of all-time, skippered the national side on a number of occasions and earned the civil honour of the MBE in 1986. Then, following a big money transfer to Derby County in June 1987, he set about creating a further series of career landmarks - he passed Terry Paine's all-time record for the highest number of League appearances with his 825th game in April 1988 and overtook Bobby Moore's record haul of England caps with his 109th selection against Denmark in June 1989. In July 1990, Shilton retired from the international scene, bowing out at the very top of his profession. He was upgraded to an OBE in 1991 and later took the plunge into management with Plymouth Argyle. Though he was initially successful, he eventually proved that he was unable to juggle the pressures of a relegation fight with those of his well-publicised personal financial difficulties and in January 1995, he resigned from Home Park after being suspended by his chairman.

He amazingly came back as a player, first with Wimbledon (no first team appearances) and then Bolton Wanderers. He became the oldest man ever to play for the club when coming on as a substitute in a 1-1 draw at Stoke and holding his place for the play-off semi-final first-leg at Wolverhampton Wanderers where he produced a sterling display in a narrow defeat. After a spell with West Ham United he joined Leyton Orient where four days before Christmas 1996, he made his 1000th League appearance in the live *Sky Sports* game against Brighton and Hove Albion and was given a special award to mark the achievement by the FA.

NIGEL SPINK

Born	8 August 1958. Chelmsford.
Career	Chelmsford City; Aston Villa (January 1977) West Bromwich Albion (January 1996) Millwall (September 1997)
Internationals	1983 v Australia (Drew 1-1)

Nigel Spink worked as an apprentice plasterer on leaving school and joined his home-town team Chelmsford City as a part-time professional. He made his debut in the Southern League at the age of 17, his displays attracting the attention of a number of leading clubs. Crystal Palace, Nottingham Forest and West Ham United all chased him, but in January 1977 the powerfully-built goalkeeper signed a five-year contract with Aston Villa, although he was fourth choice at the time behind Jimmy Rimmer, John Burridge and Jake Findlay.

He made his league debut for Villa against Nottingham Forest on Boxing Day 1979 but remarkably his next first team appearance was in the 1982 European Cup Final against Bayern Munich in Rotterdam. He had been named as substitute 'keeper that evening but after just ten minutes play, he was plunged into the deep end as Jimmy Rimmer left the field with a damaged neck. Spink played superbly and stepped up to collect his winners' medal after a Peter Withe goal had given Villa a 1-0 win.

He eventually replaced Rimmer on a permanent basis midway through the 1982-83 season and at the end of that campaign he toured Australia with England, winning his one cap when he replaced Peter

Shilton at half-time in a 1-1 draw. Injuries marred the next few seasons for him but in 1987-88 he was ever-present as Villa were promoted to the First Division. When Villa were First Division runners-up to Liverpool in 1989-90, Spink again played in every game, conceding just 38 goals. He lost his first team place to Les Sealey in 1991 but regained it a year later, playing in every game except one in the 1992-93 season. Eventually losing his place to Mark Bosnich after appearing in 461 first team games, he joined West Bromwich Albion in January 1996.

In doing so, he became at 37 years 176 days, the oldest player ever to join the Baggies' ranks ! His vast experience and presence between the posts was a great confidence booster to an Albion defence which had been flagging before his arrival. Though injuries limited his appearances for the Baggies' he acted as the club's goalkeeping coach until September 1997 when Millwall, who were short of cover for Tim Carter, paid £50,000 for his services. Though he has now turned forty, he is still an outstanding goalkeeper who commands his box, is a great shot-stopper and still has a great enthusiasm for the game.

RON SPRINGETT

Born   22 July 1935. Fulham.

Career   Victoria United; Queen's Park Rangers (February
                    1953) Sheffield Wednesday (March 1958) Queen's
                    Park Rangers (May 1967) Ashford Town (September
                    1970)

Internationals   1959 v N.Ireland (Won 2-1) 1960 v Scotland (Drew
                    1-1) v Yugoslavia (Drew 3-3) v Spain (Lost 0-3)
                    v Hungary (Lost 0-2) v N.Ireland (Won 5-2)
                    v Luxembourg (Won 9-0) v Spain (Won 4-2)
                    1961 v Scotland (Won 9-3) v Mexico (Won 8-0)
                    v Portugal (Drew 1-1) v Italy (Won 3-2) v Austria
                    (Lost 1-3) v Luxembourg (Won 4-1) v Wales (Drew
                    1-1) v Portugal (Won 2-0) v N.Ireland (Drew 1-1)
                    1962 v Austria (Won 3-1) v Scotland (Lost 0-2)
                    v Switzerland (Won 3-1) v Peru (Won 4-0) v Hungary
                    (Lost 1-2) v Argentina (Won 3-1) v Bulgaria (Drew
                    0-0) v Brazil (Lost 1-3) v France (Drew 1-1)
                    v N.Ireland (Won 3-1) v Wales (Won 4-0) 1963
                    v France (Lost 2-5) v Switzerland (Won 8-1)
                    1965 v Wales (Drew 0-0) v Austria (Lost 2-3)
                    v Norway (Won 6-1)

Ron Springett began his Football League career with Queen's Park Rangers and made his debut against Norwich City (Home 1-2) in November 1955. It was midway through the following season when he established himself as the club's permanent first team goalkeeper. His spectacular performances were soon recognised by the bigger clubs and in March 1958 he was transferred to Sheffield Wednesday.

He made his debut for the Owls against Bolton Wanderers, keeping a clean sheet in a 1-0 win. Unfortunately, despite some heroic performances he couldn't prevent Wednesday from being relegated at the end of that season.

However, he was a key member of the Owls' side that won the Second Division Championship the following season, keeping 13 clean sheets in the 32 matches in which he played. In 1959-60 he made the first of nine appearances for the Football League against the Irish League and won the first of 33 caps for England when he played against Northern Ireland. In fact, Springett still holds the record of being Sheffield Wednesday's most capped England international.

It was Springett's fine goalkeeping that kept the club in the upper reaches of the First Division for six seasons in the early 1960s and yet, though he appeared in 384 games in his nine full seasons with Wednesday, he was never an ever-present. International recognition apart, the 1966 FA Cup Final when the Owls lost 3-2 to Everton was the closest he got to glory at club level.

In 1967 he returned to Queen's Park Rangers in the unique deal which brought his brother Peter to Hillsborough, with Rangers receiving £35,000 to balance the deal. Ron Springett made a further 45 league appearances before his retirement in 1969 to take his total League and Cup appearances for the Loftus Road club to 103.

Springett, who was later involved in a gardening business, twice played in the same game as his brother Peter, once while a Wednesday player and once while with Queen's Park Rangers - the Owls won on both occasions !

ALEX STEPNEY

Born	18 September 1942. Mitcham, Surrey.
Career	Tooting and Mitcham 1958; Millwall (May 1963) Chelsea (May 1966) Manchester United (September 1966) Dallas Tornado (January 1979) Altrincham as player/coach (September 1979)
Internationals	1968 v Sweden (Won 3-1)

Of all the goalkeeper's in Manchester United's long history, Alex Stepney will always rank among the most popular and respected. A solid, secure and unspectacular 'keeper, he began his career with non-League Tooting and Mitcham before turning professional with Millwall in 1963.

He had made almost 150 appearances for the Lions when in May 1966, Tommy Docherty signed him for Chelsea for £50,000. Stepney made just one league appearance for the Stamford Bridge club before four months later being transferred to Manchester United for £55,000. At least Chelsea made a profit but given the magnificent service that

Stepney gave to United, the Blues might later have regretted not giving him a little more encouragement.

He immediately replaced Dave Gaskell in the United side and made his league debut in front of 62,085 fans in the Manchester 'derby' as a Denis Law goal gave United a 1-0 win. In his first season at Old Trafford, United lifted the League Championship and then in 1967-68, the European Cup. It was the heroics of Alex Stepney with two instinctive saves from Eusebio in the closing minutes of normal time which kept United alive in the final against Benfica. The extra-time goals will always be the highlight of the famous victory but Stepney's part should never be forgotten.

He went on to play in 535 League and Cup games for United and even scored a couple of goals from the penalty-spot in the Red's relegation season of 1973-74 - Leicester City (Home 1-2) and Birmingham City (Home 1-0) - at one point he was actually the club's leading goalscorer. He won a Second Division Championship medal to add to his League Championship medal and later won an FA Cup winners' medal when United beat Liverpool 2-1 at Wembley in 1977 to deny the Anfield club the 'double'. Stepney was capped just once by England, in 1968 against Sweden and although he was also chosen for the 1970 World Cup squad, he never actually played.

After twelve seasons' loyal service, he left United and went to play in the United States with Dallas Tornadoes and then later returned to these shores to play non-League football for Altrincham. After retiring, Stepney had a spell as commercial manager at Rochdale, having held a variety of jobs, including running a pub and working in a car body repair shop. He is now goalkeeping coach at Manchester City.

BERNARD STRETEN

Born	14 January 1921. Gillingham, Norfolk.
Died	10 May 1994.
Career	Notts County (amateur) Shrewsbury Town (amateur) Luton Town (January 1947) King's Lynn (July 1957) Wisbech Town cs 1959; Cambridge City cs 1961; North Walsham FC, Norfolk as a permit player.
Internationals	1949 v N.Ireland (Won 9-2)

After playing Norfolk junior football, Bernard Streten had a brief spell as an amateur with Notts County before joining Shrewsbury Town midway through the Second World War. Before he had even played for the Gay Meadow club, Streten 'guested' for Wolverhampton Wanderers, making four appearances in the Football League (North). His performances for Shrewsbury in the Midland League where he kept 16 clean sheets in 53 games, led to Luton Town manager George Martin securing his services for the Hatters in 1947.

A skilful, daring and often inspired goalkeeper, he made his debut in a 3-2 win over Nottingham Forest. He was ever-present in 1947-48 and at the end of the season, he signed professional forms. The following year he made his debut for England when he played against Ireland in November 1949 in a 9-2 victory. A fortnight later, he was replaced in goal by Bert Williams but was the reserve when England beat Italy 2-0. Two months later he was out of the Town team and playing in Combination football! Such was his lot at Kenilworth Road at the time. he asked for a transfer but later changed his mind and went on to prove himself a fine clubman to the Hatters.

After ten years at Kenilworth Road in which he made 301 first team appearances, he left to take over a business in Mundlesey but he was soon tempted out of retirement to play for Kings Lynn in the Midland League with other former Luton favourites, Jim Pemberton and Johnny Downie. He later played for Wisbech Town and Cambridge City before ending his career as a permit player for North Walsham in Norfolk, where he lived until his death in May 1994.

JOHN SUTCLIFFE

Born	14 April 1868. Shipden nr Halifax.
Died	7 July 1947.
Career	After a distinguished career in rugby football he joined Bolton Wanderers (September 1889) Millwall Athletic (April 1902) Manchester United (May 1903) Plymouth Argyle (January 1905) Southend United (1911/12) Arnhem (Holland) coach 1914 and had a spell as Bradford City's trainer from May 1919
Internationals	1893 v Wales (Won 6-0) 1895 v Ireland (Won 9-0)

v Scotland (Won 3-0) 1901 v Scotland (Drew 2-2)
1903 v Wales (Won 2-1)

John Sutcliffe who was the eldest of a large family, was born at Shipden near Halifax in April 1868 and was one of three players to win England honours at both rugby and soccer. He began his rugby career with Bradford before joining Heckmondwike with whom he was playing when he won an England cap against New Zealand in 1889. Towards the end of that year, Heckmondwike were suspended for professionalism and so Sutcliffe turned his attention to soccer.

He joined Bolton Wanderers to strengthen the club's forward line but in his first game for the club's Reserve side against Accrington, his rugby instincts were obvious for all to see and he switched to keeping goal. Sutcliffe made his league debut for the Wanderers in December 1889 in a 7-0 rout of West Bromwich Albion at Pikes Lane. Midway through the following season he became the club's first-choice 'keeper, a position he held for the next 11 seasons.

Sutcliffe was a good all-round sportsman, playing cricket for Great Lever CC and being the fastest player in the club over 100 and 440 yards as he proved in the club's sports day of 1890. Sutcliffe, who kept goal for the Football League on three occasions, won the first off five full caps for England in March 1893 when he played against Wales at Stoke's Victoria Ground.

In January 1902, Sutcliffe became the first Bolton Wanderers player to be sent-off at Burnden Park when he received his marching orders for dissent in a 3-1 win over Sheffield Wednesday.

After problems over wages and a benefit, Sutcliffe, who had appeared in 364 League and Cup games for the Wanderers, left the club in May 1902 to join Millwall for £400. After just one season with the London club, whom he helped to the FA Cup semi-finals, he signed for Manchester United after his request to rejoin Bolton was turned down. A year later, Sutcliffe joined Plymouth Argyle, making 166 Southern League appearances for them before becoming coach at Southend United and at Arnhem, Holland in 1914.

After the war, Sutcliffe, whose younger brother Charles kept goal for Leeds City, Rotherham and Sheffield United, was appointed trainer at Bradford City.

HARRY SWEPSTONE

Born	1 July 1859. Stepney, London.
Died	7 May 1907
Career	Clapton; Pilgrims; Ramblers; Swifts 1887-88; Also represented Essex and London; Founder member of the Corinthians, playing twice in season 1885-86. Served on the FA Committee 1883-84.
Internationals	1880 v Scotland (Lost 4-5) 1882 v Scotland (Lost 1-5) v Wales (Lost 3-5) 1883 v Wales (Won 5-0) v Ireland (Won 7-0) v Scotland (Lost 2-3)

Harry Swepstone was born in the Stepney district of London and after attending Chigwell School, began to play football for Clapton before joining the Pilgrims. His performances soon led to him winning representative honours for both Essex and London before in March 1880, he was chosen to play for England against Scotland at Hampden Park. England lost 5-4 and Swepstone was replaced by John Hawtrey for the next encounter against the Auld Enemy in 1881 but was back in the side for the 1882 game, again at Hampden Park.

This time the Scots won 5-1 but Swepstone kept his place for the game against Wales at Wrexham two days later, though he again conceded five goals as England were beaten 5-3. After keeping two clean sheets in big wins over Wales and Ireland, Swepstone made his sixth and final international appearance for England against Scotland at Bramall Lane. In a match that was almost postponed because of heavy snow, Swepstone had only himself to blame for never appearing on the winning side against the Scots. With the scores level at 2-2, Kay of Queen's Park lobbed Swepstone from fully 30 yards but as he caught the ball, he stepped back over his goal-line and the goal allowed to stand to give Scotland a 3-2 victory.

Inspite of that lapse, Swepstone was ranked as the best goalkeeper of his day, though a contemporary writer said he had a peculiar aptitude for striking the ball away with his arm!

On leaving the Pilgrims, he had spells with the Ramblers and Swifts and was a founder member of the Corinthians, responsible for giving the club its name. Swepstone, who served on the FA Committee in 1883-84 was a solicitor by profession, practising at both Bethnal Green and Bishopsgate.

FRANK SWIFT

Born   24 December 1913. Blackpool.
Died   6 February 1958.

Career   Blackpool Gasworks; Fleetwood 1931-32; Manchester
City (October 1932) 'guested' for Hamilton
Academicals during the Second World War;
Internationals 1946 v N.Ireland (Won 7-2) v Republic of Ireland
(Won 1-0) v Wales (Won 3-0) v Holland (Won 8-2)
1947 v Scotland (Drew 1-1) v France (Won 3-0)
v Switzerland (Lost 0-1) v Portugal (Won 10-0)
v Belgium (Won 5-2) v Wales (Won 3-0) v N.Ireland
(Drew 2-2) v Sweden (Won 4-1) 1948 v Scotland
(Won 2-0) v Italy (Won 4-0) v Denmark (Drew 0-0)
v N.Ireland (Won 6-2) v Wales (Won 1-0) 1949
v Scotland (Lost 1-3) v Norway (Won 4-1)

Frank Swift set the standards for goalkeeping before and after the Second World War. He signed for Manchester City from Fleetwood just before his 19th birthday and worked his way up through the 'A' team and Reserves before eventually making his league debut on Christmas Day 1933 against Derby County.

He was a superb shot-stopper, his agility, imposing physique and enormous hands made him into one of the best goalkeepers of his generation. Indeed for five years between December 1933 and September 1938, he had an amazing unbroken spell in the club's senior squad and was a member of the legendary sides that won the FA Cup in 1934 and the League Championship in 1936-37. In the final, City beat Portsmouth 2-1 but at half-time, Pompey led 1-0 with Swift conceding that he might have saved the goal had he been wearing gloves ! Fred Tilson hit two second half goals and on the final whistle, the 19-year-old Swift turned to collect his cap and gloves and fainted ! Afterwards he said 'Fancy a great strapping fellow like me fainting in front of all those people and the King.'

Frank Swift was a great character in the dressing-room, entertaining and motivating the City side with his string of impersonations and comedy turns. Even on the pitch he could fool around with the best of them. He often used to make an acrobatic dive that would have the crowd roaring even though he knew the ball was going well wide !

In 1935 he made an appearance for The Rest in a trial match against England but it was to be after the Second World War when he played in a full international. He won 19 caps for England, his first against Northern Ireland in 1946 and played in many wartime internationals. He had been skipper of Manchester City for a couple of seasons, when against Italy in 1948, he became the first goalkeeper to captain England. He had a magnificent game, one save from Gabetto the Italian centre-forward was out of this world, leaving him beating the turf with his fists!

Swift was a spectacular goalkeeper, loved by the crowd. He was daring and sometimes even headed shots away !

He finally hung up his boots in September 1949 after an illustrious career which saw him play in 376 games for the Maine Road club, paving the way for another goalkeeping legend, Bert Trautmann to step into his role.

In the 1950s, Frank embarked upon a successful career in sports journalism. However, it was while reporting on Manchester United's European Cup campaign of 1958 that he tragically lost his life in the Munich air disaster.

T

TED TAYLOR

Born	7 March 1887. Liverpool.
Died	5 July 1956.
Career	Liverpool Balmoral; Oldham Athletic (February 1912) 'guest' player for Liverpool and Fulham during the First World War; Huddersfield Town (June 1922) Everton (February 1927) Ashton National (September 1928) Wrexham (November 1928)
Internationals	1922 v Ireland (Won 2-0) 1923 v Wales (Drew 2-2) v Belgium (Won 6-1) v Scotland (Drew 2-2) v Ireland (Lost 1-2) 1924 v Scotland (Drew 1-1) v France (Won 3-1) 1926 v Scotland (Lost 0-1)

A cousin of Charlie Hallows the Lancashire and England cricketer, Ted Taylor began his league career with Oldham Athletic whom he joined for £30 from Liverpool Balmoral in February 1912.

However, due to the presence of Howard Matthews, Taylor in ten years at Boundary Park, only made 86 first team appearances for the Latics. His debut came in the final game of the 1912-13 season when he performed heroics in a goalless home draw against Manchester United. The Old Trafford club also provided the opposition when Taylor was granted a benefit match by the Latics in April 1922.

The following June, Taylor, who was a goalkeeper of real quality - quick thinking and quick moving - moved to fellow First Division club Huddersfield Town for a fee of £1,950 as a replacement for Sandy Mutch.

In 1923 and 1924, Taylor appeared alongside Huddersfield team-mate Sam Wadsworth for the Professionals against the Amateurs, in FA Charity Shield games and the Football League. Taylor was also an England regular, making the first of his eight appearances in October 1922 in a 2-0 win over Ireland at the Hawthorns. For Huddersfield, Taylor won League Championship medals in 1923-24 and 1925-26 and would have won a third but for breaking his leg against Manchester City at Maine Road in October 1924. In February 1927, Taylor, who had made 129 appearances for the Yorkshire club, was transferred to Everton and after making his debut for the Goodison club in a 1-0 defeat at Liverpool in the local derby, went on to win another League Championship medal in 1927-28 at the age of 41.

On leaving the Toffees he had a spell with Ashton National before ending his league career with Wrexham. Although standing only 5ft 8 ins, Taylor, who was considered one of the best goalkeepers of his time, later went into the cotton trade in Manchester.

GEORGE TOONE

Born	10 June 1868. Nottingham.
Died	1 September 1943.
Career	Nottingham Jardine's; Notts Rangers; Notts County 1889; Bedminster (August 1899) Bristol City cs 1900; Notts County cs 1901;
International	1892 v Wales (Won 2-0) v Scotland (Won 4-1)

George Toone was born in Nottingham in 1868 and played with several local teams, notably Nottingham Jardine's and Notts Rangers before joining Notts County in 1889. He helped them win the Second Division title in 1896-97 after winning an FA Cup winners' medal in 1894 as they beat Bolton Wanderers 4-1. This made up for the disappointment of missing the 1891 final through injury when Notts County lost 3-1 to Blackburn Rovers.

It was whilst with County that Toone won his two England caps against Wales and Scotland in 1892 when he was on the winning side both times.

In 1899 he moved to Bedminster and when they amalgamated with Bristol City in 1900, he became a Babes' player. He had been Bedminster's regular 'keeper and in his one season with City he was ever-present as the club finished the campaign as runners-up in the Southern League. The Bristol Observer once described George Toone as being 'without doubt one of the best conducted professional players in the West'.

In 1901-02 Toone returned to Notts County where he remained until retiring at the end of the 1902-03 season.

Father of George junior a half-back with Notts County, Sheffield Wednesday and Watford, George Toone was a Nottingham licensee for a number of years after leaving the game.

DAN TREMELLING

Born	12 November 1897. Burton-on-Trent.
Died	15 August 1970.

Career	Langworth Colliery Junction Wagon Works;
	Shirebrook; Lincoln City during the First World
	War; Birmingham (June 1919) Bury (May 1933)
	Had a spell as Birmingham's assistant-trainer
	from June 1936 to the Second World War.
Internationals	1927 v Wales (Lost 1-2)

Dan Tremelling took up goalkeeping by accident after being placed there during an injury crisis at Langwith. He later played for Shirebrook Juniors before turning professional with Lincoln City at the end of the First World War. His outstanding performances for the Imps prompted Birmingham to sign him and he made his debut for the Blues in a 4-1 home win over Hull City on the opening day of the 1919-20 season. Tremelling was the club's only ever-present during a campaign in which he kept 17 clean sheets.

The following season he won a Second Division Championship medal. An ever-present in seasons 1923-24 and 1924-25, Tremelling missed very few games in twelve seasons with the St Andrew's club and was responsible for Cardiff City not winning the League title in 1923-24 - he saved Len Davies' last-minute penalty-kick which had he scored, would have given the Bluebirds the First Division Championship.

CARRERAS CIGARETTES

D. TREMELLING
BURY (2ND DIVISION)

Affectionately known as the 'India Rubber Man' due to him continually bouncing around on his line, Tremelling was an utterly reliable and sometimes absolutely brilliant goalkeeper who was a great catcher of the ball. He was also a perfectionist and was rumoured to have gone into hiding for a few days after some poor displays ! Tremelling won just one England cap, playing in a 2-1 defeat by Wales at Turf Moor in 1927 though he did represent the Football League on three occasions.

He played in 395 League and Cup games for Birmingham before losing his place to Harry Hibbs, who had been on the Blues' books for five years before establishing himself as the club's first-choice 'keeper. After a spell with Bury, Dan Tremelling, whose brother Bill won honours with Blackpool and Preston North End, returned to St Andrew's to become the club's trainer, a position he held for three years until the outbreak of the Second World War.

HUGH TURNER

Born	6 August 1904. Wigan.
Died	16 May 1997.

Career	Felling Colliery (Darlington on amateur forms cs 1924) High Fell FC cs 1925; Huddersfield Town (April 1926) Fulham (May 1937)
Internationals	1931 v France (Lost 2-5) v Belgium (Won 4-1)

Though he was rather small for a goalkeeper, Wigan-born Hugh Turner was described by the Topical Times as 'a smart 'keeper who had inspired days when he could not be rivalled, as well as fine agility and anticipation'.

Turner began his career with Felling Colliery in Darlington whom he joined in the summer of 1924. He later joined the town's Division Three (North) club but after failing to make their league side, he left to play for the Northern Alliance side High Fell of Gateshead. It was from here that he joined Huddersfield Town in April 1926.

Although arriving at Leeds Road immediately after the Yorkshire club's triple Championship successes and missing the 1928 FA Cup Final, he did play in the 1930 Final which Town lost 2-0 to Arsenal. Between April 1928 and March 1932, Turner appeared in 181 consecutive League and Cup games.

In May 1931 he gained England caps against France and Belgium, replacing the injured Harry Hibbs and later that year, represented the Football League against the Irish League at Blackpool's Bloomfield Road ground.

Turner gave the Terriers great service, making 394 League and Cup appearances in eleven seasons with the club before leaving in June 1937 to play for Fulham.

Replacing the Cottagers' regular 'keeper Alf Tootill, he was ever-present in Fulham's last full season, 1938-39 before World War Two and after playing in three League South 'B' matches for the Craven Cottage club, he retired.

GEORGE TWEEDY

Born	8 January 1913. Willington, Co Durham.
Died	23 April 1987.
Career	Willington Town; Grimsby Town (August 1931)
	Grimsby Town assistant-manager (September 1950)
	returned as a player late in 1951, finally
	retiring in April 1953.
Internationals	1936 v Hungary (Won 6-2)

Arguably the best goalkeeper ever to play for Grimsby Town, George Tweedy joined the Mariners from the Durham club, Willington Town as an 18-year-old in 1931. After some impressive displays for the Blundell Park club's reserve side, he made his League debut in November 1932 against Bradford City when the Mariners' regular 'keeper Tommy Read broke a finger.

He played in the next nine games but then lost his place when Read regained full fitness. Tweedy returned to the first team for a brief spell midway through the 1933-34 season before establishing himself as the club's first-choice 'keeper at the start of the following campaign.

An ever-present in seasons 1934-35 and 1936-37, Tweedy made the first team spot his own, missing just seven league games in the five seasons prior to the outbreak of the Second World War.

His consistency during this period led to him winning full international honours for England when on 2 December 1936 he made his only appearance in a 6-2 win over Hungary at Highbury. There is no doubt that but for the presence of Harry Hibbs and Vic Woodley, his international career would have been much longer.

At the outbreak of war, Tweedy continued to keep goal for the Mariners, making 56 appearances over three seasons. Later during the hostilities, he 'guested' for both Hibernian and Arsenal, in each case just missing playing in a War Cup Final because of military postings.

When league football resumed in 1946-47, Tweedy was still the club's number one 'keeper and played on until 1950 before retiring to become the Mariners' assistant-manager. When Stan Hayhurst broke his finger in the opening game of the 1951-52 season, Grimsby manager Bill Shankly persuaded Tweedy to don the jersey again and he made a further 32 league appearances for the club before finally retiring. He played the last of his 372 League and Cup games for the Mariners against York City on Good Friday 1953, when he was 40 years of age.

Settling in the Grimsby area, George Tweedy, one of the many Tynesiders to have found his way to Blundell Park, later became engaged in the furniture trade.

W

TONY WAITERS

Born	1 February 1937. Southport.
Career	RAF Football (Middlesbrough amateur) Loughborough College; Bishop Auckland; Macclesfield; Blackpool (October 1959) Retired May 1967 on appointment as FA North-West regional coach; Liverpool coach (January 1969) Burnley player/coach (July 1970) Coventry City director of coaching (December 1971) Plymouth Argyle manager (October 1972) Vancouver Whitecaps manager cs 1977; Coach to Canadian Olympic games team 1984; He also had spells as Tranmere Rovers coach and as a Chelsea scout.
Internationals	1964 v Republic of Ireland (Won 3-1) v Brazil (Lost 1-5) v Belgium (Drew 2-2) v Wales (Won 2-1) v Holland (Drew 1-1)

Tony Waiters won England Amateur honours whilst at Loughborough College and then played for Bishop Auckland and Macclesfield before joining Blackpool in October 1959. Scottish international 'keeper George Farm had been a permanent fixture between the posts for the Bloomfield Road club for well over a decade but Waiters set about replacing him, making his debut in a 1-0 win over Blackburn Rovers on Boxing Day 1959.

After that the first team jersey was his though he did have to fight off another future England goalkeeper in Gordon West.

Waiters was a fitness fanatic and worked consistently at developing and improving his skills. He won his first representative honour in October 1963 when he played for the Football League against the League of Ireland in Dublin. Then in May 1964, he won the first of five full caps for England, also in Dublin, performing well in a 3-1 victory over the Republic of Ireland. His second international appearance was a week later in the Maracana Stadium in Rio de Janeiro and with Pele in outstanding form, Waiters could do little to prevent the Brazilians from winning 5-1.

All his Blackpool career was spent in the top flight but after the Seasiders were relegated in 1966-67, Waiters, who had played in 286 games for the Bloomfield Road club, decided to retire - he was just thirty. He was a firm favourite with the Blackpool fans but in eight seasons with the club, he enjoyed none of the top honours - maybe it was this that persuaded him to retire so early !

He became the Football Association's North West Regional Coach, later joining Liverpool as the Anfield club's youth coach.

In July 1970 he joined Burnley as a coach, also acting as understudy to the Clarets' regular 'keeper Peter Mellor. Within a couple of weeks, Mellor had dislocated his shoulder and so Waiters stepped up to resume his First Division career at the age of 33. In his Burnley debut against Liverpool he was penalised for taking too many steps, following the rule change in the summer. The Reds scored as a result of the free-kick and went on to win 2-1.

Waiters was Burnley's regular goalkeeper until December 1971 when he retired once more to join Coventry City as Director of Coaching.

After a spell as England Youth Team Manager he spent five years as manager of Plymouth Argyle, guiding them to the semi-final of the League Cup in 1974 and to promotion from the Third Division in 1975.

Following a number of successful years as coach of Vancouver Whitecaps in the NASL, Waiters was appointed as coach to the Canadian National Team, leading them to the 1986 World Cup Finals in Mexico.

IAN WALKER

Born	31 October 1971. Watford.
Career	Tottenham Hotspur (December 1989) Oxford United on loan (August 1990)
Internationals	1996 v Hungary (Won 3-0) v China (Won 3-0) 1997 v Italy (Lost 0-1)

Ian Walker joined Tottenham Hotspur's trainee staff having graduated from the FA's School of Excellence at Lilleshall. England's regular 'keeper from Under-15 through to Under-19 level he helped the Spurs' youth team win the FA Youth Cup in 1990 but with Erik Thorstvedt, Bobby Mimms and Gareth Howells all his senior, he began the 1990-91 season out on loan with Oxford United and later Ipswich Town.

Without having made a first team appearance for the White Hart Lane club, Walker made his debut for the England Under-21 side against Wales in December 1990. Walker made his league debut for Spurs against Norwich City in April 1991, a match the Canaries won 2-1. Sitting on the Norwich bench was his father Mike, the former Watford and Colchester United goalkeeper who was then on the club's coaching staff. In August 1991, Walker made his second first team appearance, replacing Thorstvedt, who was away on international duty and kept the big Norwegian out on merit until he was taken ill.

A goalkeeper with a cool temperament, Walker has been Spurs' first-choice custodian for the last nine seasons, his consistency helping him become a regular in the England squad. At his best when displaying the agility and quick reflexes which have become his trade mark at White Hart Lane, his confidence took something of a knock when conceding seven goals against Newcastle United and six in the League Cup at the hands of First Division champions, Bolton Wanderers. Also, he received media-wide criticism for his part in Zola's goal in England's 1-0 defeat against Italy in the World Cup qualifier at Wembley.

Happily since then, Walker has regained his confidence and has grown in ability to organise his defence. Now looking far more confident and asserting that confidence over his back four, Ian Walker, who reaped enormous benefit from the coaching of former England 'keeper Ray Clemence in his early days has now appeared in over 300 first team games for Spurs.

CONRAD WARNER

Born	19 April 1852. Cripplegate, City of London.
Died	10 April 1890.
Career	Upton Park (Captain and President in the mid 1880s). Played for London and Middlesex in representative matches.
Internationals	1878 v Scotland (Lost 2-7)

Conrad Warner came from a wealthy Quaker family and was educated at Grove House School in Tottenham. He was a games' all-rounder, assisting Chestnut Rugby Union club in the early 1870s, captaining Southgate hockey club and was sometime secretary of the Winchmore Hill Cricket and Lawn Tennis club.

In terms of football, Warner was looked upon as the best goalkeeper of his period and after representing London and Middlesex, made his full international debut for England against Scotland at Hampden Park in March 1878. In a game played in muddy and slippery conditions, the England goal was under constant pressure as Scotland won a one-sided match 7-2. Warner's club side were Upton Park and for a number of years in the 1880s, he was both captain and President.

The Football Annual for 1881 describes Warner as 'a capital goalkeeper, always cool and very quick at getting rid of the ball. However, at that time he was not devoting so much of his leisure to the game and was concentrating more on his vocation as a stationer with Partridge and Cooper, a firm still in existence today. He died of pneumonia in New York in April 1890 at the age of thirty-eight while on a business trip there.

REGINALD de COURTNEY WELCH

Born	20 June 1851. Kensington, London.
Died	4 June 1939.
Career	Harrow School (XI in 1871) Old Harrovians; Harrow Chequers; Wanderers; Remnants; Also represented Middlesex and served on the FA Committee 1873-1875 and 1879-1880.

Internationals   1874 v Scotland (Lost 1-2)

Having attended Harrow School where he was a member of the school's first XI, he began his playing career with Old Harrovians before moving on to play for a number of clubs.

His first appearance for his country came in the very first official England v Scotland international on 30 November 1872 when the two countries played out a goalless draw at the West of Scotland Cricket Club in Partick. However in that game, he played at full-back where his accurate kicking led to a number of chances being created for the visitors' forwards. Though he wasn't as good between the posts, he was England's custodian in the 1874 Scotland match, again at the West of Scotland Cricket Club, which the home side won 2-1. By this time, Welch was playing for Harrow Chequers, having won his first cap whilst with the Wanderers.

Welch won two FA Cup winners' medals with the Wanderers as they beat the Royal Engineers 1-0 in 1872 and Oxford University 2-0 in 1873.

Welch, who also represented Middlesex, served on the FA Committee from 1873 to 1875 and from 1879 to 1880.

From 1883 to 1895 he was employed as an Army tutor, subsequently becoming Principal of the Army College, Farnham, Surrey.

GORDON WEST

Born   24 April 1943. Darfield nr Barnsley.

Career   Blackpool (April 1960) Everton (March 1962)
                    Tranmere Rovers (October 1975)
Internationals   1968 v Bulgaria (Drew 1-1) 1969 v Wales (Won 2-1)
                    v Mexico (Drew 0-0)

Despite being born near Barnsley, Gordon West began his Football League career with Blackpool as a 17-year-old, making his debut in a 3-1 defeat at Bolton Wanderers in January 1961. A little over a year later, he was on his way to Everton as Blues' manager Harry Catterick paid 27,500 to secure his services. It was then a record fee for a goalkeeper but it paid immediate dividends as West replaced Albert Dunlop and helped the Blues take the League Championship in his first full season at

Goodison Park. Over the next three seasons, Andy Rankin sometimes claimed his place but when Everton won the FA Cup in 1966, beating Sheffield Wednesday 3-2, West was in goal.

West was an instinctive performer and courageous at close-quarter blocks; he was also breathtaking as a shot-stopper. One weakness that the Everton goalkeeper did possess was a rather inadequate kick - a legacy of a long-standing thigh injury - but the big 'keeper compensated amply with constructive throws in the style of Manchester City's Bert Trautmann.

After fighting off the challenge of Andy Rankin, West missed only a handful of games and picked up a second League Championship medal in 1969-70.

West endeared himself to the Kopites after reacting to one of their customary fusillades of abuse by blowing them a kiss; their response was to present him with a handbag ! Yet despite his ebullient personality, Gordon West was notoriously nervous before a game.

In the late sixties he made three appearances for England, the first against Bulgaria as understudy to Gordon Banks but he surprised the football world by declining to join the World Cup squad in Mexico 1970 - Stepney was picked instead.

Though he was dropped in favour of Rankin in 1970-71, West fought back and in 1971-72 was ever-present. He left Goodison Park in 1973 after appearing in 399 League and Cup games for Everton, though there were many who believed the 30-year-old was retiring prematurely. Their contention proved to be right when two years later he was lured back to the game by Tranmere Rovers, playing in 17 league games as well as providing four seasons of first team cover.

Across the Mersey, Everton were not to find a truly satisfactory replacement for West until the arrival of Neville Southall.

LEONARD WILKINSON

Born	15 October 1868. Highgate, London.
Died	9 February 1913.
Career	Charterhouse School (XI in 1887) Oxford University (Blue 1889-90-91) Old Carthusians; Corinthians (1890-1893)

Internationals   1891 v Wales (Won 4-1)

On leaving Charterhouse where in 1887 he had been a member of the school's first XI, he went up to Oxford University. As well as gaining a Blue in football in each of his three years at Oxford, he also gained a Blue in athletics in 1890 and 1891.

In March 1891, Wilkinson won his only full cap for England when he played against Wales at Roker Park. Alongside him in the 4-1 win was his Oxford University team-mate, full-back Elphinstone Jackson.

Wilkinson, who also played for the Old Carthusians along with fellow internationals Hugh Stanbrough and Charles Wreford-Brown, shared the distinction of appearing in all three of Old Carthusians' FA Amateur Cup Finals of the 1890s, being on the winning side on two occasions.

A top-class amateur 'keeper Leonard Wilkinson, who was lithe in movement and capable of brilliance, also represented the Corinthians.

On hanging up his boots, Wilkinson worked as a barrister, having been called to the Bar in 1893.

BERT WILLIAMS

Born   31 January 1920. Bilston.

Career   Thompson's FC (Wolverhampton Works League)
                Walsall (April 1937) Wolverhampton Wanderers
                (September 1945)

Internationals 1949 v France (Won 3-1) v Republic of Ireland
                (Lost 0-2) v Wales (Won 4-1) v Italy (Won 2-0)
                1950 v Scotland (Won 1-0) v Portugal (Won 5-3)
                v Belgium (Won 4-1) v Chile (Won 2-0) v United
                States (Lost 0-1) v Spain (Lost 0-1)
                v N.Ireland (Won 4-1) v Wales (Won 4-2) v Yugoslavia
                (Drew 2-2) 1951 v Scotland (Lost 2-3) v Argentina
                (Won 2-1) v Portugal (Won 5-2) v France (Drew 2-2)
                v Wales (Drew 1-1) 1954 v West Germany (Won 3-1)
                1955 v Scotland (Won 7-2) v France (Lost 0-1)
                v Spain (Drew 1-1) v Portugal (Lost 1-3) v Wales
                (Lost 1-2)

B ert Williams was Wolves' first-choice goalkeeper from September 1945
until April 1957, a total of twelve seasons. During that time he
appeared in 448 matches - the most by any 'keeper registered with the
Molineux club.

Bilston-born Williams played for Thompson's FC after leaving school
and in April 1937 he signed as an amateur for Walsall, taking professional status at Fellows Park in March 1939.

During the Second World War he saw a lot of the world while serv-
ing in the RAF and when the hostilities ended, he joined Wolves in
September 1945 for a bargain £3,500. He made his league debut for
Wolves in a 6-1 home win over Arsenal on the opening day of the 1946-
47 season. One of the greatest names in the history of Wolverhampton
Wanderers, he won an FA Cup winners' medal in 1949 as Leicester City
were beaten 3-1 and followed that up by earning a First Division
Championship medal in 1953-54.

Quite brilliant at times, agile, alert and utterly reliable, Bert Williams,
affectionately known as 'the Cat' was without doubt England's top
'keeper in the early part of the 1950s. Winning a total of 24 caps for
his country, he made his international debut three weeks after winning
his FA Cup winners' medal as England beat France 3-1 in Paris. His final
appearance came six years later in October 1955 as England lost 2-1 to
Wales at Ninian Park. Williams was also England's World Cup 'keeper
in 1950 and he finished up on the losing side in only seven of all the
internationals he played in.Williams, who also played in the 1954 FA
Charity Shield game against West Bromwich Albion at Molineux, a

match which ended all-square at 4-4, finally retired at the end of the 1956-57 season, handing over to Malcolm Finlayson. He became a business man and ran a highly successful sports outfitters in his home-town of Bilston for a number of years as well as a goalkeeping school.

ERNEST WILLIAMSON

Born	24 May 1890. Murton Colliery, Co Durham.
Died	30 April 1964.
Career	Murton Red Star (Wearside League) Wingate Albion (North Eastern League) Croydon Common (June 1913) Army Football; Arsenal cs 1919; Norwich City (June 1923)
Internationals	1923 v Sweden (Won 4-2) v Sweden (Won 3-1)

Ernest Williamson began his goalkeeping career in North Eastern junior football, first with Murton Red Star and then Wingate Albion before moving south to London to join Croydon Common in the summer of 1913.

His performances for the Southern League Second Division club attracted the attention of a number of top clubs and just when it seemed as if he would be given the chance at Football League level, the First

World War interrupted his progress. During the hostilities, Williamson 'guested' for Arsenal in 122 matches as well as serving in the RASC.

He officially signed for the Gunners for a fee of £150 in April 1919 and in 1919-20 the first season of peacetime football, he played in 26 league games. By the end of that campaign, he had become the Highbury club's first-choice 'keeper, a position he held for the next three seasons. This consistency led to him becoming Arsenal's first England international after the First World War when he won two caps against Sweden.

However, after conceding fourteen goals in the first five games of the 1922-23 season he lost his place to Stephen Dunn and later John Robson and having appeared in 113 League and Cup games, he was transferred to Norwich City in June 1923.

Williamson spent two seasons at Carrow Road before retiring to become a licensee in Norwich for a good many years.

TIM WILLIAMSON

Born	6 June 1884. North Ormesby, Yorkshire.
Died	1 August 1943.

Career	Redcar Crusaders; Middlesbrough (1903)
Internationals	1905 v Ireland (Drew 1-1) 1911 v Ireland (Won 2-1)
	v Wales (Won 3-0) v Scotland (Drew 1-1) 1912
	v Wales (Won 2-0) v Scotland (Drew 1-1) 1913
	v Ireland (Lost 1-2)

An Ayresome Park institution for over twenty years, Tim Williamson first appeared for Middlesbrough in a friendly match against Cliftonville after impressing for Redcar Crusaders. His display in the friendly match was outstanding but Williamson would only sign professional forms for the north-east club if they agreed to allow him to continue qualifying as a draughtsman!

Thankfully, the Middlesbrough board agreed and Williamson made his Football League debut in a 2-0 home win over Bristol City in April 1902. It was midway through the following season before he established himself as the club's first-choice 'keeper - a position he held until the end of the 1922-23 campaign.

Williamson won seven full caps for England, the first against Ireland at Ayresome Park in February 1905. The match ended all-square at 1-1 with Williamson scoring the Irish side's goal!

He was ever-present in five seasons for Middlesbrough - 1903-04, 1906-07, 1908-09, 1909-10 and 1920-21. With the exception of his first two games for the club, Williamson played all his football in the First Division, appearing in 563 league games. In all he appeared in 602 first team games and scored two goals, both from the penalty-spot against Liverpool (Home 2-2 April 1910) and Bristol City (Home 3-0 September 1910).

A man of great character and deservedly popular everywhere, he played, Williamson was a great 'keeper. A contemporary wrote of his ".....keen perception and remarkable agility and his advice and instruction to the young players with whom he is surrounded has proved a big asset to the north-eastern club."

RAY WOOD

Born	11 June 1931. Hebburn Co Durham.
Career	Darlington (September 1949) Manchester United (December 1949) Huddersfield Town (December 1958) Bradford City (October 1965) Barnsley (October 1966) Los Angeles Wolves manager (January 1968) later coached in Cyprus, Greece, Kuwait and Kenya. From 1978 was coach to the Emirites Sports Club, Abu Dhabi and their national side.
Internationals	1954 v N.Ireland (Won 2-0) v Wales (Won 3-1) 1956 v Finland (Won 5-1)

Born at Hebburn-on-Tyne, Ray Wood was another of the fine players from the north-east who joined Manchester United in the 1940s. He had been a professional goalkeeper with Darlington for only six months when United signed him as an 18-year-old in December 1949. He stepped straight into the first team against Newcastle United for whom he had played as an amateur, the day after he signed but despite having a good game in a 1-1 draw it was the only game he was to play for a number of seasons.

Wood was basically used as cover for Jack Crompton but following the signing of Reg Allen, he had to be content with Central League football. It was not until late 1952 that he was to get a second chance but after that his appearances were more regular until he became first choice in the 1953-54 season.

Wood was a member of United's 1955-56 and 1956-57 League Championship winning sides, but he is probably best remembered however for the 1957 FA Cup Final when he was injured following a collision with Aston Villa's Peter McParland. Wood's cheekbone was broken and he was stretchered off the field with Jackie Blanchflower forced to take over in the United goal. Wood returned later to play on the wing and then back in goal but he was a mere passenger, still dazed from the heavy collision. It was to be the pinnacle of Wood's United career.

Less than a year later, he crawled out of the wreckage of the crashed BEA Elizabethan Airliner at Munich and by the time he had recovered from his injuries, Irish international Harry Gregg had claimed the goalkeeper's jersey. Wood played just one more game for the Reds to take his total of League and Cup appearances to 205 before being sold to Huddersfield Town in December 1958. He enjoyed a long career with the then Leeds Road club, appearing in 207 league games before having spells with Bradford City and Barnsley.

After that he took up an appointment as manager of Los Angeles and then as manager of the national Cyprus team. After spells coaching in Greece, Kuwait and Kenya, he became coach to the Emirites Sports Club, Abu Dhabi and their national side before ending his involvement with the game.

VIC WOODLEY

Born	26 February 1910. Slough.
Died	23 October 1978.
Career	Windsor and Eton (Spartan League) Chelsea (May 1931) Bath City (December 1945) Derby County (March 1946) Bath City player-manager (May 1947)
International	1937 v Scotland (Lost 1-3) v Norway (Won 6-0) v Sweden (Won 4-0) v Finland (Won 8-0) v Ireland (Won 5-1) v Wales (Won 2-1) v Czechoslovakia

(Won 5-4) 1938 v Scotland (Lost 0-1) v Germany
(Won 6-3) v Switzerland (Lost 1-2) v France (Won
4-2) v Wales (Lost 2-4) v FIFA (Won 3-0) v Norway
(Won 4-0) v Ireland (Won 7-0) 1939 v Scotland
(Won 2-0) v Italy (Drew 2-2) v Yugoslavia (Lost
1-2) v Romania (Won 2-0)

Vic Woodley had played for Chippenham and Windsor and Eton but it
was whilst playing for the Athenian League against the Berks and
Bucks in 1931 that he was spotted by Chelsea and Aldershot. Offered a
trial by both clubs, he chose to join Chelsea but must have thought he was
in for a long stay in the Stamford Bridge club's reserves as at that time
Chelsea's first-choice 'keeper was the Scottish international Johnny Jackson. However, Woodley's undoubted ability was quickly spotted by manager Leslie Knighton and in August 1932 he made his league debut, going
on to be a fixture in Chelsea's goal throughout most of the 1930s.

He played four times for the Football League in 1937 and 1938 and
won his first England cap against Scotland at Hampden Park in April
1937. He kept his place in the England side until the outbreak of the
Second World War. During that time, he made 19 consecutive international appearances, the best sequence recorded until Ron Springett
passed it in the early 1960s.

He continued to appear in the Wartime and Victory internationals
and played for Chelsea in the Football League (South) Cup Final in
1944. Woodley, who had appeared in 252 league games for the
Pensioners, was released from Stamford Bridge in December 1945 and

joined Bath City on loan.

Derby County gave Woodley an unexpected chance to crown his distinguished career. Following an injury to Frank Boulton, the Rams needed an experienced goalkeeper for their FA Cup campaign. County manager Stuart McMillan negotiated with Chelsea who still held Woodley's registration and with Bath City, for whom he was playing at the time. He played in the semi-finals where players reckoned his superb save from Harold Bodle in the replay against Birmingham City at Maine Road kept them in the Cup and in the Wembley victory when the Rams beat Charlton Athletic 4-1. He stayed with Derby for the following season, making 30 league appearances before rejoining Bath City where he later became player-manager.

Woodley, who had no pretensions towards showiness, meeting all demands with impressive assurance, later became a licensee at Bradford-on-Avon in Wiltshire where he died.

CHRIS WOODS

Born	14 November 1959. Boston.
Career	Nottingham Forest (December 1976) Queen's Park Rangers (July 1979) Norwich City (March 1981) Glasgow Rangers (June 1986) Sheffield Wednesday (August 1991) Reading on loan (October 1995) Southampton (November 1996) Sunderland (March 1997) Burnley (July 1997)
Internationals	1985 v United States (Won 5-0) 1986 v Egypt (Won 4-0) v Israel (Won 2-1) v Canada (Won 1-0) 1987 v Yugoslavia (Won 4-1) v Spain (Won 4-2) v N.Ireland (Won 2-0) v Turkey (Won 8-0) v Scotland (Drew 0-0) 1988 v Israel (Drew 0-0) v Hungary (Drew 0-0) v Switzerland (Won 1-0) v USSR (Lost 1-3) 1989 v Denmark (Drew 1-1) 1990 v Brazil (Won 1-0) v Denmark (Won 1-0) 1991 v Hungary (Won 1-0) v Poland (Drew 1-1) v Republic of Ireland (Drew 1-1) v USSR (Won 3-1) v Australia (Won 1-0) v New Zealand (Won 1-0) v New Zealand (Won 2-0) v Malaysia (Won 4-2)

1992 v Germany (Lost 1-2) v Turkey (Won 1-0)
v Poland (Drew 1-1) v France (Won 2-0) v CIS
(Drew 2-2) v Brazil (Drew 1-1) v Finland (Won 2-1)
v Denmark (Drew 0-0) v France (Drew 0-0) v Sweden
(Lost 1-2) 1993 v Spain (Lost 0-1) v Norway
(Drew 1-1) v Turkey (Won 4-0) v San Marino (Won
7-1) v Turkey (Won 2-0) v Holland (Drew 2-2)
v Poland (Won 3-0) v Norway (Lost 0-2) v United
States (Lost 0-2)

Nottingham Forest beat a number of other clubs for the signature of this promising young 'keeper. He sprang to fame in 1977-78 when Forest, newly promoted to Division One, ran away with the League Championship. However, he played no part in that particular triumph but starred in the club's first-ever League Cup victory. The club's number one 'keeper Peter Shilton was ineligible for the League Cup having played in the competition for Stoke City and so Woods played in every match from the third round through to the Cup Final. One of the youngest and certainly least experienced players to appear in a Wembley Cup Final. After making a great save from Kenny Dalglish in the first minute, he performed impeccably and helped Forest win 1-0 in a replay after a goalless draw at Wembley. The following season he was selected for the England Under-21 team - the first player to be so honoured without a Football League appearance to his name.

Clearly too good a player to remain as Peter Shilton's understudy, he was allowed to join Queen's Park Rangers in the summer of 1979 and made his Football debut on the opening day of the 1979-80 season, keeping a clean sheet in a 2-0 win over Bristol Rovers. An automatic choice for one and a half seasons at Loftus Road, he inexplicably lost his place to John Burridge and in the summer of 1981, was sold to Norwich City.

Ever-present in four of his five seasons at Carrow Road, he won a second League Cup winners' medal in 1984-85 when the Canaries beat Sunderland 1-0. At the end of the season on tour with the England team, he won his first cap against the United States. Although they were relegated in 1984-85, Norwich came back as Second Division champions at the first attempt but Woods did not stay for the next stint of top flight football, being one of the first England internationals to join the exodus to Graeme Souness' Glasgow Rangers team.

In five years at Ibrox Park, he won four Scottish League Championship medals and four Skol League Cup medals and never lost his place except for injuries. However, in 1991, Rangers reduced their contingent of English players to avoid problems with the UEFA ruling on 'foreigners' in European competition and he was sold to newly promoted Sheffield Wednesday for £1.2 million.

In his first season at Hillsborough, the Owls finished third and almost 'stole' the League Championship 'at the death'. In 1992-93 he kept 13 clean sheets including three in a row and helped the Yorkshire club to both the FA and League Cup Finals. After that he began to have a bad time with injuries and lost both his Sheffield Wednesday and England place but after the Owls lost 7-1 to Nottingham Forest, he regained his place and signed a new contract. He had a brief loan spell with Reading but on his return to Hillsborough with Pressman injured, he stepped up to play well, showing flashes of his old brilliance before injury ruled him out too.

He left Sheffield Wednesday during the 1996 close season for a stint in the United States but came back in November to replace Southampton's out-of-favour Dave Beasant, playing in six games before breaking a leg at Blackburn Rovers.

On recovering from the injury, he joined Sunderland on a short term contract in March 1997 as cover for Lionel Perez. When the Wearsiders released him, he joined Burnley where playing in a side facing relegation, he proved that much of his old ability was still in place, producing an amazing double save against Grimsby Town. At the end of the 1997-98 season, Woods left Turf Moor after injuries had forced him to retire.

Top Tens

To qualify for inclusion in the lists below, a goalkeeper has had to appear in at least 10 full internationals. In the early days of international football, the matches were few and far between and the custodian changed regularly with no-one making more than a few appearances. The first goalkeeper to qualify was Jack Robinson who appeared in 11 games between 1897 and 1901.

MOST APPEARANCES

1.	Peter Shilton	125
2.	Gordon Banks	73
3.	Ray Clemence	61
4.	David Seaman*	52
5.	Chris Woods	43
6.	Ron Springett	33
7.	Harry Hibbs	25
8.	Bert Williams	24
9.	Gil Merrick	23
10.	Sam Hardy	21

MOST APPEARANCES WITH ONE LEAGUE CLUB

1.	Ray Clemence	Liverpool	55
2.	David Seaman*	Arsenal	49
3.	Peter Shilton	Southampton	49
4.	Gordon Banks	Leicester City	37
5.	Gordon Banks	Stoke City	36

6.	Peter Shilton	Derby County	34
7.	Ron Springett	Sheffield Wednesday	33
8.	Harry Hibbs	Birmingham City	25
9.	Bert Williams	Wolves	24
10.	Gil Merrick	Birmingham City	23

PERCENTAGES OF MATCHES IN WHICH CLEAN SHEETS WERE KEPT

1.	David Seaman*	55.76%
2.	Chris Woods	53.48%
3.	Peter Shilton	52.00%
4.	Gordon Banks	47.94%
5.	Frank Swift	47.36%
6.	Jack Robinson	45.45%
7.	Ray Clemence	44.26%
8.	Harry Hibbs	38.46%
9.	Vic Woodley	36.84%
10.	Sam Hardy	33.33%

NUMBER OF GOALS CONCEDED PER GAME

1.	David Seaman*	0.59
2.	Peter Shilton	0.67
3.	Chris Woods	0.72
4.	Gordon Banks	0.78
5.	Tim Flowers	0.81
6.	Frank Swift	0.89
7.	Ray Clemence	0.91
8.	Jack Robinson	1.00
9.	Harry Hibbs	1.04
10.	Sam Hardy	1.19

* still playing for England.